Advice from the Attic

Perilous Pearls of Wisdom
on
Beauty, Charm and Etiquette

Monica Dale

Hatpin Press

Published by Hatpin Press
Ellicott City, Maryland 21042

ISBN 0-9701416-3-7

Library of Congress Control Number: 2002110520

DISCLAIMER:

This book is intended to entertain and inform
readers with obsolete advice found in antiquated
sources. Excerpts are presented for reading only.
This book is not intended to provide practical advice, and should not be used as such.

Do not implement the ideas and advice in this
book. If you take any action based on this book, you
do so at your own risk. The author and publisher do
not assume responsibility for any damage, harm or
injury caused by or related to advice, techniques, ingredients, or ideas described in this book.

In other words, *don't try this at home!*

What people are saying about
Advice from the Attic. . .

"*Advice from the Attic* kept me in stitches from the moment I began reading it ~ especially Monica's previews before each chapter... This is a great read for anyone who needs to lighten up."

– Joyce Weiss, author of *Take the Ride of Your Life*

"Witty, ridiculous ~ what were they thinking. Then again, is it rude to clutch yourself and laugh hysterically at some of this nonsense? Maybe I should look that up too!"

– Kitty Werner, author of *The Savvy Woman's Guide to Owning a Home*

"This collection of snippets would do well to sit on anyone's coffee table to provide hours of illuminating and amusing topics of conversation... A fun book that provides many a smile and shrug of disbelief, *Advice from the Attic* is the perfect gift for a girlfriend or a pick-me-up for a blue day."

– Denise M. Clark, *Denise's Pieces Book Reviews*

"In these days of spas and facials and mud baths and massages, we don't have to suffer to be beautiful, at least not like our turn-of-the-century (the last century, that is) counterparts did, if one believes *Advice from the Attic: Perilous Pearls of Wisdom on Beauty, Charm and Etiquette*, a charming and clever (and just a little ironic) new book by Monica Dale about the suffering of our antiquarian counterparts.

Advice from the Attic is a funny and clever and enlightening collection of (not-so) antiquated advice."

- Elizabeth Cone, *The Betsy-Tacy Society*

"*Advice from the Attic* is a fun and useful read that proves that the quest for beauty is timeless."

- Diane Irons, author of *Bargain Beauty Secrets*

"As sisters in the perpetual pursuit of fierceness, we know a thing or two about the lofty price of beauty, the importance of a hip-ass combo, and the tragedies one suffers when painting by numbers according to Tammy Faye Baker. *Advice from the Attic* should be required reading for every maiden Drag Queen who has ever fallen prey to the ridiculous notion of applying antiperspirant to one's face, or using an outdoor adhesive to secure one's 'Oh my Jesus' eyelashes."

- Dragness Morehead

Contents

Acknowledgements

Many thanks to my sisters, Karen, Lesley and Melissa, for encouraging me to create this book and advising me along the way; to my husband Michael, for putting up with the book collection that's taken over our house; to Kitty Werner, for answering all my emails with supportive assistance; and to my daughter Hilary, for cataloguing the sources and for being her free-spirited self. May she never take silly advice seriously.

This book is dedicated to my mother

Claire Marie Christy Dale

in loving memory.

Introduction

History is fascinating.

Oh, I'm not talking about the history we learned in high school – I fell asleep listening to lectures on wars.

The history that fascinates me gives authentic little glimpses into how people lived the simplest aspects of their lives. I raised my hand to ask obscure questions. How did people wash their clothes and raise their children? Did they vote, work, and travel? What thoughts occupied their minds, what worries burdened their psyches, what tasks consumed their time?

It seems to me that mundane matters and simple day-to-day endeavors speak more intimately and eloquently about people's lives than do the larger issues of their government recounted by traditional history.

A particularly addictive peek into the thoughts of people past comes from what they read. I purchased my first antiquarian book on etiquette years ago, and was hooked immediately. I confess—it was all downhill from there. The next thing I knew, I was cruising the internet trolling for old beauty books and hanging out in dirty auction houses. And no intervention could save me.

I started turning other people on to my odd obsession, casually passing favorite passages around at parties. My friends wanted more, and soon they pressed me to compile my wildest excerpts into a book. To stretch the metaphor tighter than a bad face lift, with this book I've become a bonafide dealer.

Antiquated advice written directly to women lets us taste of a small part of our foremother's lives. It's a chance to put ourselves in their place, and try as best we can to imagine their thoughts and perspectives. Yet who knows what they really thought of the advice to stay quiet, singe their eyelashes, and bathe with ammonia?

I imagine their responses ranged from earnest study to loud laughter, much as we react to the extremes of social mores, beauty advice and product infomercials that confront us today .

But let's not entirely emulate the trusting readers of past generations. There was quite a bit of advice they took seriously that's downright dangerous. Mercury, arsenic, and kerosene were just a few of the ingredients recommended for beauty preparations. I've omitted the most deadly potions and notions here—for example, a five-day face peel that causes swollen-shut eyes and instructions for gasoline shampoo (despite its warnings not to apply friction or smoke during the process).

So this book comes with a warning its predecessors did not: don't try any of this at home! These pages are meant to entertain you, not to harm you. I don't really know what would happen if you put horseradish on your hands, bathed in ammonia, or tried burning your eyelashes, but let's not find out.

And while the advice on social behavior isn't quite so dangerous, people will certainly wonder about you if you begin speaking oddly, staring into space, or working too hard at placing your posterior into a chair. (And if you insist on performing the nude "Charleston Twist" exercise, for heaven's sake, close the blinds first!)

Better simply to read, enjoy, and be happy we've progressed beyond these pages. We can certainly be glad the days of fussing and fretting over our behavior, words, hair, weight, and complexion are over.

Or are they?

Charm

The word "charm" has come to connote graceful allure, polished poise, and the skills of perfectly refined flirtation. But the core definition of charm involves supernatural power and magical enchantment

The magic of feminine "charm" was apparently anything but natural, and involved tactics far trickier than any sleight-of-hand. The pursuit of charm required the discipline to practice the proscribed choreography for sitting in a chair, cultivate the properly placid facial expression, and endure any pain to acquire correct posture. Women were also admonished not to move too much, speak too loudly, or show too much intelligence. Don't laugh—that was considered improper, as well!

Charm went beyond the social graces required for acceptance in polite society: it was a necessity for enticing a suitable husband. Apparently, men of earlier eras enjoyed the company of silent, stone-faced, not-too-smart women who didn't laugh much. (It seems the Stepford Wives had ancestors.)

But many suitors did expect a musical audition. For decades, no self-respecting middle class family was without a pianoforte. Even here, women were warned to play down their abilities, and of course, to avoid unnecessary movement and facial expressions.

(If Botox had been around in those days, every woman of the aristocracy would have been properly and perpetually paralyzed.)

For those who did heed the unfortunate requirements of charm, we need only remove the "c" from the word to understand what it must have done to the joy and spirit of their lives.

We can only hope that some of these "charming" women got together for the occasional wild quilting bee, free to sing, shout, and make all sorts of improper facial expressions — and, of course, laugh their heads off!

Charm Defined

You must learn to look attractive in repose, to stand and walk gracefully, to sit in or rise from a chair with charm. The proper position of the hands and the feet must add to your appearance. You must know how to go up or down a flight of stairs beautifully, how to enter a room and how to say good-bye, and how to use your eyes most effectively.

Marianne Meade
Charm and Personality (1938) 3

If you would gather the roses of charm... you must look fresh and dainty, the sight of you must gladden the eye, the sound of your voice must enchant the ear, the touch of your hand must thrill.

Harriet Lane
The Book of Culture (1922) 11-12

She must cease frowning and learn to smile; she must repress anger and resentment, and turn the other cheek; she must not seek favors, but discover the joy of bestowing blessings on others...

T.W. Shannon
Perfect Womanhood (1913) 73-74

I'm sure you're smiling *now* just for the joy of knowing that you have at last found something that is going to make you a new woman; not the *mannish* new woman about whom we have heard so much, nor the new woman with all the sweetness crushed out; but the sweet, pure, healthy, wholesome and fascinating woman with more of love and sympathy — the dainty woman whom everybody loves.

I want you to begin at once — this very evening — to attain the innocent charms so dear to the true, womanly woman.

Alice M. Long
My Lady Beautiful (1906) 36-39

Intelligence

Young men like to talk about themselves. If you wish to be popular with them, this is worth bearing in mind.

Frederick H. Martens
The Book of Good Manners (1923) 116

Never talk much when you are in the company of men. Let them lead the conversation... The clever woman never talks about herself to a man whom she desires to interest.

Monsieur Georges A. Sakele
One Thousand and One Beauty Hints (1931) 16

Every woman now-a-days is expected to be generally well-informed, but a strong woman is an abomination.

A Society Lady
How to Acquire Personal Beauty (1889) 97

Men want women to depend upon them, to have need of their counsel... Keep it quiet that you can add and subtract, that you play a top game of golf. Play down your accomplishments at times.

Edyth Thornton McLeod
Your Home Guide to Health, Beauty, Charm (1947) 59

Conversation has its place;
   But, if you gaze out into space;
   Deep mystery will surround you.
   Men will love it, too.

Donna Louise Hoffer
How to Be A Fashion Model (1940) 34

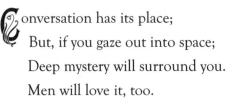

One does not wish to hear a lady talk politics nor a smattering of science; but she should be able to understand and listen with interest when politics are discussed, and to appreciate in some small degree the conversation of scientific men.

Author Unknown
The Standard Book on Politeness (1884) 38

Facial Composure

T here is a way also of looking that must be regu-
lated. The audacious stare is odious; the sly,
oblique, impenetrable look is unsatisfactory. Softly
and kindly should the eyes be raised to those of the
speaker, and only withdrawn when the speech, whatever it may be, is concluded. Immediate intimacy
and a familiar manner are worse than the glum look
with which some young ladies have a habit of regard-
ing their fellow mortals.

Henry Davenport Northrop
The Household Encyclopedia (189?) 23

I ndulge in no facial contortions, as they rapidly
become habits difficult to break and usually leave
their traces on the face in lines impossible to efface.
Lifting the eyebrows, rolling the eyes, opening them
very widely, twisting the mouth and opening it so as
to show the tongue in talking, are all disagreeable
habits, that, once acquired, can only be broken by
ceaseless vigilance.

Maud C. Cooke
Manual of Social Forms (1896) 46

Repose is the proper state of beauty. Repose of feature and a gentle self-command are most grievously needed by the American young woman... Her childhood is almost entirely unfamiliar with the governing discipline of English and Continental children in the same station; and so she grows to womanhood over-exhilarated, loud-voiced, and *risque*. She giggles and wriggles and twists, until every feature is distorted and every curve, in what might be a shapely little body, is deformed. No race of girls, on the face of the earth, giggle so honestly, so incessantly, and so purposelessly as the American. The risible muscles, constantly in motion, give to a face the broad, grinning visage of harlequin, or the intemperate leer of a bacchante, utterly destroying the pathetic poise of countenance, that is only the result of pure principles and gentle meditations.

Annie Wolf
The Truth About Beauty (1892) 74-75

outh mannerisms are leaks of beauty. Self-conscious young women draw down the corners of their mouths when they talk or when they smile. They twist one corner of the mouth downward, making the mouth one-sided. They even suck their lips inward, spoiling the contour of the mouth. They rub their faces with nervous fingers. They elevate one eyebrow and pull down the other.

Mme. Lina Cavalieri
My Secrets of Beauty (1914) 93

y the way, I wonder if you squint just a wee bit, especially when you are facing the bright sunlight; and I wonder, too, if you curl up your nose something like a cunning little rabbit. Of course, it looks just "too cute for anything" when bunny does it, but, oh, dear, you are not a rabbit and that makes all the difference in the world.

Alice M. Long
My Lady Beautiful (1906) 96

Movement

Let your carriage be at once dignified and graceful. There are but a few figures that will bear quick motion; with almost every one its effect is that of a jerk, a most awkward movement. Let the feet, in walking or dancing, be turned out slightly; when you are seated, rest them both on the floor or a footstool. To sit with the knees or feet crossed or doubled up, is awkward and unlady-like. Carry your arms, in walking, easily; never crossing them stiffly or swinging them beside you. When seated, if you are not sewing or knitting, keep your hands perfectly quiet. This, whilst one of the most difficult accomplishments to attain, is the surest mark of a lady. Do not fidget, playing with your rings, brooch, or any little article that may be near you; let your hands rest in an easy, natural position, perfectly quiet.

Florence Hartley
Ladies' Book of Etiquette (1873) 151

ow many women know how to walk? Observe them on the street or entering a drawing-room — even the better classes. One shambles, another slouches, as if her shoes — yes, and her stockings too — were down at the heels. But most of them drive, straining every muscle in their sweet bodies, ploughing along with strenuous effort like a ship in a high sea, and facing head winds. Five minutes' instruction in stage-walk, properly observed, would rectify every bit of this. A perceptible swing of the entire body should be manifest with every step. That is, advance all of one side, with a slight turn right and left of the shoulders, as the corresponding foot is projected.

Annie Wolf
The Truth About Beauty (1892) 61-62

any dames, by not bending the knees, render their walk very ungraceful.

Author Unknown
The Bazar Book of Decorum (1870) 102

Walk up to the chair. When you reach it, one foot should be in front of the other, the length of a step apart. Rise slightly on the balls of both feet, and turn your back to the chair without lifting either foot completely off the floor. Now bend the knee which is nearest the chair (the other knee will bend slightly also, but you needn't pay much attention to this one), and lower yourself lightly into the chair, remembering always to keep the upper part of the body erect. Do not allow your feet to take a side-by-side position, or you will find yourself assuming the modified jack-knife pose which is so awkward. With practice, the three steps — approaching the chair, turning on the balls of the feet, and lowering your body into the chair — should be accomplished as one graceful movement, with no pauses.

Marianne Meade
Charm and Personality (1938) 87

While some never fairly get on a seat but to their own manifest discomfort and that of all who look upon their misery... there are others who roll their bodies into heaps, as it were, and throw them with an audible bounce deep into the receptacle, whatever it may be.

Author Unknown
The Bazar Book of Decorum (1870) 103

Posture

The arms hang naturally from the shoulders, the hands are in some quiet position, the fingers curve gracefully, with slight partings between the first and second, and the third and fourth. There is no stiffness, no uneasy shifting or fidgeting, no moving of fingers or features, but all is rounded and graceful as a statue. It is worth some pains to be a lady of good standing in society.

Monfort B. Allen and Amelia C. McGregor
The Glory of Woman (1896) 446-447

Ladies should never adopt the ungraceful habit of folding their arms, or of placing them akimbo.

Annie Randall White
Twentieth Century Etiquette
(1903) 339

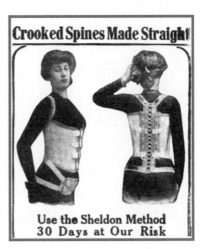

Crooked Spines Made Straight

**Use the Sheldon Method
30 Days at Our Risk**

If you are inclined to stoop, walk to and fro with your hands behind your back when you are alone in the garden or house.

Charles Morris, Ed.
The Standard Book of Etiquette (1901) 76

Recently I, who rail at everyone about these things, fell from grace...

I was sewing (that's a dark secret) when my friend's husband said: "I say, Jo, that's a graceful foot pose you have! Is THAT one of your Secrets of Charm?" I looked down to find my left ankle bent into a most awkward position! Naturally I straightened out the foot, and you can rest assured that it remained straight for the rest of the evening!

Josephine Huddleston
Secrets of Charm (1929) 246

Knock-Knees. — A correspondent says: "I commenced the practice of placing a small book between my knees, and tying a handkerchief tight round my ankles. This I did two or three times a day, increasing the substance at every fresh trial, until I could hold a brick with ease breadth-ways. When I first commenced this practice I was as badly knock-kneed as possible; but now I am as straight as any one. I likewise made it a practice of lying on my back in bed, with my legs crossed and my knees fixed tightly together. This, I believe, did me a great deal of good."

Mrs. Jane Warren
Ladies' Own Home Cook Book (1891) 118

ow are you sitting right now as you read this? Dollars to doughnuts you're slumped down in your chair, sitting halfway between your neck and what you were given to sit upon. Or else you've got one hip up in the air and legs hiked out of sight. Oh, I know you. And do you think that's pretty? It's terrible, and I want you to stop it right now, do you hear?

Sylvia of Hollywood
Streamline Your Figure (1939) 114

nly self-control and gumption will get those shoulders up and keep them up... find a friend who when she finds you slumping will give you a good, hard whack between your shoulder blades. Tell this friend to give you one you won't forget in a hurry. That will remind you if you can't remind yourself.

Sylvia of Hollywood
No More Alibis! (1934) 67

Music

Never exhibit any anxiety to sing or to play. You may have a fine voice, have a brilliant instrumental execution, but your friends may by possibility neither admire nor appreciate either.

Emily Thornwell
The Lady's Guide to Perfect Gentility (1856) 97

There are many young women, who, when they sit down to the piano to sing, twist themselves into so many contortions, and writhe their bodies and faces about into such actions and grimaces, as would almost incline one to believe that they are suffering great bodily torture. Their bosoms heave, their shoulders shrug, their heads swing to the right and left, their lips quiver, their eyes roll; they sigh, they pant, they seem ready to expire!

Richard A. Wells
Manners, Culture and Dress (1891) 389

It is a misfortune of musical people generally to be such enthusiasts, that once beginning they seldom know when to leave off; there are few things a greater seccatura than a long "Concerto," or duett upon the pianoforte, or an "Air with (endless) variations."

Author Unknown
The Standard Book on Politeness (1884) 32

Page after page of black, closely printed notes, will drive those who see them from the piano. They may be executed in the most finished style, but they are not suited to general society...

Avoid the loud, thumping style, and also the over-so-solemn style...

Avoid movement at the piano. Swinging the body to and fro, moving the head, rolling the eyes, raising the hands too much, are all bad tricks, and should be carefully abstained from.

Florence Hartley
Ladies' Book of Etiquette (1873) 189

Virtue and Modesty

A lady should never seem to understand an indelicate expression, much less use one.

Emily Thornwell
The Lady's Guide to Perfect Gentility (1856) 110

A woman is not supposed to recognize a man who is one of a group standing in a public place, since a modest girl will not look close enough at a group of men to recognize an acquaintance.

N.C.
Practical Etiquette (1899) 134

The woman who has a divine sex appeal is the one who blushes after displaying her calves and quite naturally makes it apparent that she is embarrassed.

John Hewins Kern
Glorious Womanhood (1925) 52

You should sit very properly at your desk or in any other place, not immodestly crossing your legs in such a way that those around you make remarks about your physical charms. When you sit with your dress above your knees you invite familiarity, and you needn't be offended when it confronts you. You should be careful that your dress is not too low in the neck. You often invite insult and criticism by carelessly stooping in a dress which permits only an erect position.

Sophia C. Hadida
Manners for Millions (1935) 263-264

Keep good company or none. You can always have books if you cannot have people.

Mortimer Chesterfield
Etiquette for Every Occasion (1916)
148

Vice and Immodesty

The hoiden is defined to be a rude, rough, romping girl. The term will apply to such as are not restrained by the rules of polite society to be courteous and civil, but are continually planning and performing unmaidenly actions. A kind of independence which asserts itself in always doing right, is not the kind that charms the hoiden. She delights to indulge in violations of propriety, which sometimes shock and always annoy her more discreet companions. Such a character is not the one that wins commendation, much less admiration and respect, from good society. Young men may appear to enjoy her company, but she can never be regarded with that high esteem which arises from confidence in her modesty and reliance upon her good sense.

Monfort B. Allen and Amelia C. McGregor
The Glory of Woman, (1896) 499

I t is generally in this class that we find young girls who prefer, to an altogether unreasonable and unbecoming extent, the society of young men to the society of their own sex. It is among these that we find the young lady who does not know how to prevent undue familiarity in the conduct of young men; who will tolerate, without disapprobation or protest, rude conduct on the part of young men. This over-eagerness for their society, and easy toleration of too familiar conduct and conversation, young men, who are quick discerners in such matters, are very apt to take advantage of. Only the best and most high-principled among them will refrain from doing so.

Helen Ekin Starrett
The Charm of Fine Manners (1920) 65

 ay I say right here that a woman loses her modesty when dancing.

John Carrara
Enemies of Youth (1939) 24

T he modern sex dance with its close posture, its "jungle" jazz, its darkened rooms, hip flasks and late hours, makes no contribution to purity, but, rather, fires the passions.

Clayton F. Derstine
Paths to Beautiful Womanhood (1944) 85

We don't say there is no excuse for drunkenness. But certainly there is no possible hint of charm in that state.

Alice Thompson and Helen Valentine
Better Than Beauty: A Guide to Charm (1938) 147-148

A young girl who is impertinent or careless in her demeanor to her mother or her mother's friends; who goes about without a chaperon and talks slang; who is careless in her bearing towards young men, permitting them to treat her as if she were one of themselves; who accepts the attention of a young man of bad character or dissipated habits because he happens to be rich; who is loud in dress and rough in manner — such a young girl is "bad society," be she the daughter of a senator or a butcher.

Georgene Corry Benham
Polite Life and Etiquette (1902) 77

It is, moreover, a paltry ambition, and not without risk to virtue, to aspire to the distinction of being pointed out as "the low-necked" Bel Smith, or the "high-stepping" Fanny Jones, or the girl who drank a whole bottle of Champagne, or she who smoked one of Frank Tripup's fifty-cent regalias.

Author Unknown
The Bazar Book of Decorum (1870) 118

Young women, too regardless of consequences, sometimes thoughtlessly turn coquettes, present their charms and bright attractions, use their best endeavors, exhibit excessive devotion and exclusive affection, and by these means decoy and lead astray, if not absolutely ruin, many an honest, worthy young man. The hearts of such ladies exist but in name; they have long since been dissipated in thin air...

Monfort B. Allen and Amelia C. McGregor
The Glory of Woman (1896) 33-34

The coquette should remember that, with every successive flirtation, one charm after another disappears, like the petals from a fading rose, until all the deliciousness of a fresh and pure character is lost.

Charles Morris, Ed.
The Standard Book of Etiquette (1901) 265

Laughter

And as to laughter! If only young people knew what a revealer of secrets the laugh is they would, as Emerson says, "keep these entertaining explosions under strict control." The young person who laughs loudly and keeps on laughing; who cannot stop the cachinations caused by an amusing incident or story, especially if the incident relates to or the story is related by the person who laughs, betrays almost total lack of culture.

Helen Ekin Starrett
The Charm of Fine Manners (1920) 113-114

Be very careful to guard against over much laughing. Nothing gives a sillier appearance than spasms of laughter upon the slightest provocation. It soon grows into a very disagreeable habit. Smile frequently, if need be, but be moderate in laughter. A very little reasoning will serve to do this; and the reflection that few grown people laugh well will aid still farther in curbing the propensity.

Maud C. Cooke
Manual of Social Forms (1896) 48

The Folly of Laughter — True wit or sense never yet made anybody laugh; they are above it; they please the mind and give a cheerfulness to the countenance. But it is low buffoonery or silly accidents that always excite laughter; and that is what people of sense and breeding should show themselves above... Not to mention the disagreeable noise that it makes, and the shocking distortion of the face that it occasions.... I am neither of a melancholy nor a cynical disposition; and am as willing and as apt to be pleased as anybody; but I am sure that, since I have had the full use of my reason, nobody has ever heard me laugh.

Lord Chesterfield
Letters, Sentences and Maxims (n.d.) 139-140

Learn when and how to weep. It can be very charming.

Monsieur Georges A. Sakele
One Thousand and One Beauty Hints (1931) 16

Etiquette

A recent study revealed that most Americans find their counterparts lacking in manners, even downright rude. But perhaps the rudeness of society, like the insolence of adolescence, is a phenomenon continually rediscovered as if it were an entirely new, modern development.

Recorded history and literature tell us that rudeness has always been part of human behavior. (And can we really imagine that in the days before written documentation, cavemen were polite to one another? As in, "Pardon me, but would you be so kind as to allow me to drag you by the hair to my cave, for given such consent, I won't have to use this club?")

Some of the etiquette advice from the past seems absurd today. It was considered scandalous to chew gum, whistle, or smoke in public — well, sometimes history does repeat itself.

We have to wonder, however, what on earth people were doing that prompted some of the advice found. Based on the admonishments in this chapter, it seems that women brought lizards to movie theatres, put their cigarettes out in men's coffee cups, and made an awful lot of "disagreeable noises."

On the other hand, following some of the etiquette advice provided would hardly pass muster with today's Miss Manners. According to sources quoted, for example, one should not offer to treat at a restaurant, should not apologize after breaking the hostess's Ming vase, and should tell lies in order to keep the children away at dinner parties.

Other advice, such as the treatise on movie theatre etiquette, holds perfectly true today. But no one can preach it with quite the style of a judgmental 1930's matron!

So read on — but first, spit out your gum and put that lizard away.

Etiquette Defined

To look steadily at any one, especially if you are a lady and are speaking to a gentleman; to turn the head frequently on one side and the other during conversation; to balance yourself upon your chair; to bend forward; to strike your hands upon your knees; to hold one of your knees between your hands locked together; to cross your legs; to extend your feet on the andirons; to admire yourself with complacency in a glass; to adjust, in an affected manner, your cravat, hair, dress, or handkerchief; to remain without gloves; to fold carefully your shawl, instead of throwing it with graceful negligence upon a table; to fret about a hat which you have just left off; to laugh immoderately; to place your hand upon the person with whom you are conversing; to take him by the buttons, the collar of his cloak, the cuffs, the waist, etc.; to seize any person by the waist or arm, or to touch their person; to roll the eyes or to raise them with affectation; to take snuff from the box of your neighbor, or to offer it to strangers, especially to ladies; to play continually with your chain or fan; to beat time with the feet and hands; to whirl round a chair with your hand; to shake with your feet the chair of your neighbor; to rub your face or your hands; wink your eyes; shrug up your shoulder;

stamp with your feet &c.; — all these bad habits, of
which we cannot speak to people, are in the highest
degree displeasing.

Emily Thornwell
The Lady's Guide to Perfect Gentility (1856) 87-88

I n spite of certain evidence to the contrary, well-
bred people do not maul each other.

Margery Wilson
Charm (1930) 3

What belongs to the toilet should never be done in public. One may repair an accident, put up a stray ringlet, arrange a shawl, tie a string; but one may not comb the hair, clean the nails, or touch the nose or ears. It is not delicate to scratch one's self. Only under the most urgent necessity can one blow her nose in company. It may be wiped, not blown, if it can be avoided, especially at table...

Try to free yourself from all annoying habits. Do not make disagreeable noises, nor any noises that can be avoided, in eating or drinking. Never hum or whistle, unless quite alone. To do either in company may be very disagreeable. Beware of sniffing, or any unpleasant sound of nose, or mouth, or breathing. Sleep with your mouth closed, so as to never snore.

Monfort B. Allen and Amelia C. McGregor
The Glory of Woman (1896) 451

No really cultivated girl will, for instance, open and play upon a piano in a hotel parlor or any other parlor when it is occupied by strangers. She will never perform in public any of the duties of the toilet, such as cleaning her nails or using a tooth-pick. She will not eat peanuts or fruit or candy, or chew gum, in public places. In fact, I cannot imagine a really refined young lady chewing gum even in the privacy of her own room, so offensive is it to good taste. She will not descant upon bodily ailments in the drawing-room or at the table. She will not rush noisily up and down stairs or through the house, clashing doors and startling everyone with unpleasant noises. She will not interrupt people who are conversing, to ask an irrelevant question or one pertaining to her own affairs. She will not slap an acquaintance familiarly on the shoulder, or make special displays of affection or intimacy before people. She will if possible suppress the sudden sneeze, and use every effort to quiet a cough.

Helen Ekin Starrett
The Charm of Fine Manners (1920) 78-79

On the Street

The true lady walks the streets unostentatiously and with becoming reserve. So long as she maintains this character she is sacred from insult or injury, even by the rudest. She recognizes acquaintances with a courteous bow, and friends with a word of greeting. She appears unconscious of all sights and sounds which a lady ought not to perceive.

Walter R. Houghton et. al.
American Etiquette and Rules of Politeness (1884) 103

Your conduct on the street should always be modest and dignified. Ladies should carefully avoid all loud and boisterous conversation or laughter and all undue liveliness in public.

B.G. Jefferis and J.L. Nichols
Search Lights on Health (1902) 59

A woman NEVER SMOKES ON THE STREET.

Author Unknown
Good Manners (1930) 35

In the Theatre

Never read aloud anything on the screen. Take it for granted that all around you can read. As no one needs your assistance, it is very annoying to have it thrust upon him.

Never repeat after the speakers in a movie a joke or any other remark. Everyone else has heard as well as you. Your speaking disturbs. The idea that you alone see the point to the joke is one of colossal conceit.

Don't whistle, sing, hum, or tap the tunes familiar to you. Whistling causes a breeze to blow on the back of the neck of the person in front of you, and he may take cold. Singing, humming, and tapping, as well as whistling, are diverting to the attention and therefore annoying.

Wiggling the head or the shoulders to show your marvelous sense of rhythm and that you recognize the familiar tunes that, of course, everyone else recognizes, is in poor taste. Such acts rank you with the show-off. Then, too, the wigglers are usually out of rhythm. This makes them the butt of ridicule...

Don't explain the picture, as it moves along, to the child who is with you. Nine times out of ten he will be better off without the explanation. Anyway, you disturb others when so doing. A child too young to understand should not go to movies, and a child who understands should be kept at home.

Sophia C. Hadida
Manners for Millions (1935) 186

he theatre is not a boudoir, and a vanity bag is *not* — if you would rather be really well-bred than conform to a vulgar but widely prevalent belief — a theatre-seat accessory. Nor — as some young girls do — is it good form to carry small animal pets, guinea-pigs, lizards and the like, in the pocket of your cloak or wrap.

Frederick H. Martens
The Book of Good Manners (1923) 297

At the Table

K nives were made for cutting, and those who carry food to their mouths with them, frequently cut their lips.

A Lady of New York
Etiquette for Ladies (1843) 49

B lowing the nose is not a pleasant demonstration at any time, and at the table is simply unpardonable.

Agnes H. Morton
Etiquette (1895) 189

A delightful old gentleman said the reason he never married was that he watched the young woman to whom he had made up his mind to propose, eat a peach, and she spit the pit out. That finished his ambitions in that direction, and he said he didn't care to have any more illusions vanquished in this manner, so gave up all hopes of the fair sex for fear he should again be disappointed.

Ellye Howell Glover
"Dame Curtsey's" Book of Etiquette (1930) 54

W hen sipping a liquid such as soup, do it QUIETLY. Do not give anyone a chance to say or think, "I HEAR you like your soup."

Author Unknown
Good Manners (1930) 19

Should you have the misfortune, at a dinner or evening party at the house of another, to break anything which you take up, or to throw down a waiter loaded with splendid cut-glass, you should not make an apology, or appear the least mortified, or indeed, take any notice whatever of the calamity. If you exhibited any regret on such an occasion, you would seem to indicate that the loss was of importance to your entertainer, — an exceedingly poor compliment.

"A Gentleman"
The Laws of Etiquette (1844) 205

Will a good psychiatrist please take time off in the near future and try to find out why women love to put out their cigarettes in the man's coffee cup? It seems to be a universal habit, crossing racial, religious, political, economic, and geographic lines. Is it an instinct? Is it a conspiracy of some sort?

Thomas D. Horton
What Men Don't Like About Women (1945) 69

Do not pick your teeth, or plunge your finger into your mouth.

Do not play with your knife and fork, fidget with your salt-cellar, balance your spoon on your tumbler, or make pills of your bread.

James E. Homans
New American Encyclopedia (1905) 508

Signals at the Table

1. Drawing napkin or handkerchief through the hand — I desire to converse (by signal) with you.
2. Unfolding and holding it by corners - Is it agreeable?
3. Playing with fork, and holding forefinger of left hand to left ear — I have something to tell you privately.
4. Holding up knife and fork in each hand — When can I see you?
5. Laying knife and fork together on left of plate — After the meal. (This signal will suffice for query or answer.)
6. Clenched right hand on table — To-night.
7. Napkin or handkerchief held with three fingers — Yes.
8. Held with two fingers showing — No.
9. Holding napkin to chin with forefinger over mouth — Cease signaling.
10. Standing the knife and fork thus, V — Can I meet you?
11. Laying knife and fork thus, X — I am angry, or displeased.
12. Balancing fork on edge of cup — Are you engaged tonight?
13. Folding napkin triangularly (laying it down) — Have you been out since last meal?
14. Drawing knife through prongs of fork — I shall remain at home to-night.
15. Striking fork with knife — I shall go out.
16. Balance fork on knife — Meet me (or if by gentleman), Can I meet you?

17. Placing knife over the glass — Will you be alone?
18. Balancing spoon on edge of cup — I have an engagement.
19. Stirring the spoon in cup slowly — Will you be late?
20. Holding the spoon over cup and gazing meditatingly on it — We are suspected, or we are discovered.
21. Slapping the ear as if brushing away a fly — I do not understand.

Author Unknown
How to Woo and How to Win (1919) 55-56

inkling and trifling with knives and forks, rolling crumbs, marking hieroglyphics on the table cloth, patting down the salt, or shaking the ice in a tumbler are all ugly habits that can be easily overcome.

Margaret Watts Livingston, et al
Correct Social Usage (1906) 57-58

Chewing Gum

 adies do not chew gum...

Utley E. Crane, Ed.
New Outline of Knowledge, Vol. X, (1936) 139

any women believe that chewing gum will keep them from developing double chins. But if it is chewed for beautifying purposes, doesn't that place its use in the bedroom and bathroom? Since it is offensive to most people, it should never be used in public.

Margery Wilson
The Pocket Book of Etiquette (1940) 41

ever chew gum in a public place. Never chew gum in the presence of those who do not indulge in this plebeian habit.

If you disregard this suggestion, at least keep away from others. Do not stand so close that the other person must hear you chew or endure the odor...

To chew gum in public classifies you as ordinary. If you do not believe this, observe the chewers in the street cars.

Sophia C. Hadida
Manners for Millions (1935) 113-114

Miscellaneous Manners

D o not whistle when playing cards. You may blow the other fellow's cards out of his hand.

Sophia C. Hadida
Manners for Millions (1935) 162

I f you wish to make a private call upon the President, you will find it necessary to secure the company and influence of some official or special friend of the President. Otherwise, though you will be readily admitted to the White House, you will probably fail in obtaining a personal interview.

Author Unknown
Decorum (1880) 241

E conomy is nothing to be ashamed of. Avoid the habit of so-called treating. Your money goes, and you get no thanks for it. The habit is a bad one, and is closely allied with loafing and dissipation.

Georgene Corry Benham
Polite Life and Etiquette (1902) 86

Don't let one day pass without a thorough cleansing of your person.

Don't sit down to your evening meal before a complete toilet if you have company.

Don't cleanse your nails, your nose, or your ears in public.

Don't use hair dye, hair oil or pomades.

Don't overdress yourself or walk affectedly.

Don't whistle in public places, nor inside of houses either.

Don't use your fingers or fists to beat a tattoo upon floor, desk, or window panes.

Don't drink spirits; millions have tried it to their sorrow.

B.G. Jefferis and J.L. Nichols
Search Lights on Health (1902) 58-59

 lady should not cross the legs in company.

Margaret Sangster
Good Manners for All Occasions (1904) 143

on't use *hair dye, hair oil* or *pomades.*

Don't walk with a slovenly gait.

Don't carry your hands in your pockets.

Don't laugh boisterously.

Don't have the habit of "grinning." A smile or laugh is proper in its place.

Don't use a forced, light laugh in conversation.

Don't gape in company.

Don't be over-familiar.

Don't drink any alcoholic liquors of any kind whatever. It may be good etiquette to do so under certain conditions, but is not wise.

T.W. Shannon
Eugenics (1919) 51-52

f you should happen to be blessed with those lovely nuisances, children, and should be entertaining company, never allow them to be brought in after dinner, unless they are particularly asked for, and even then it is better to say that they are at school.

"A Gentleman"
The Laws of Etiquette (1844) 156

Persons who live absolutely alone in a house, apartment hotel suite, or boarding house should watch themselves very carefully. Habits that are distasteful to others are most easily developed.

Belching should be avoided when living alone for fear of forming the habit to such an extent that it cannot be controlled when around others.

Talking to one's self is a bad habit because one is likely to indulge in it when walking on the street.

Carelessness in one's appearance should be avoided because when one lives alone there is no one to go to the door to meet an unexpected guest. The habit, too, is not a desirable one.

Eating in a way offensive to others, picking bones, making noises with the mouth, disregarding rules of table etiquette — all of these violations done in the privacy of one's own home cause one to commit errors when in company and evoke such remarks as "I don't think she has a nice personality."

Sophia C. Hadida
Manners for Millions (1935) 76

Speech

ere we find all sorts of advice on how to speak and what to say — and of course, what not to say and how not to say it.

We've all heard the words, "Don't you speak to me in that tone of voice, young lady!" In these pages, that phrase takes on new dimensions. Much Victorian ink was spilled describing the importance of the proper tone of voice. Advice included everything from scolding about "yammering" to a strange little affirmation for chanting each day.

In addition to speaking properly, a well-bred woman studied the fine art of conversation. It seems she needed the help. Based on the advice given, she was apparently kept silent for so long that when called upon to converse, she blurted out the details of Uncle Ed's appendectomy in a loud, nasal tone while spraying her companions with every consonant.

Vocabulary was another area for study and improvement. Women were warned against using the term "ma'am" and the phrase "pleased to meet you." A long list of forbidden slang words must have been quite effective, because today no one's ever heard of most of them. (Try to translate: "The yappy frails jawed about the spiffilicated stew bum." And no, it's not Edward Lear.)

Of course, no proper lady uses profanity, even today. But did you know that even the term "goodness" was considered profane?

Oh yes, there's a lot to learn about speech from these experts of yesteryear.

And how did their readers feel about the mandate to be self-consciously careful of every little sound that came forth from their lips?

Who knows... They couldn't say.

Proper Speech Defined

void a muttering, mouthing, stuttering, droning, guttural, nasal, or lisping, pronunciation.

Let your speech be neither too loud nor too low; but adjusted to the ear of your companion. Try to prevent the necessity of any person crying, "What? What?"

Avoid a loquacious propensity; you should never occupy more than your share of the time, or more than is agreeable to others.

Beware of such vulgar interpolations as "You know," "You see," "I'll tell you what."

Pay a strict regard to the rules of grammar, even in private conversation. If you do not understand these rules, learn them, whatever be your age or station.

Though you should always speak pleasantly, do not mix your conversation with loud bursts of laughter.

Never indulge in uncommon words, or in Latin and French phrases, but choose the best understood terms to express your meaning.

Above all, let your conversation be intellectual, graceful, chaste, discreet, edifying, and profitable.

Florence Hartley
Ladies' Book of Etiquette (1873) 152-153

o, when you talk, keep your hands still.

Do try to be sensible; it is not a particular sign of superiority to talk like a fool.

Do be reticent; the world at large has no interest in your private affairs.

Maud C. Cooke
Manual of Social Forms (1896) 172-174

n hearing some of our damsels speak, we are forcibly reminded of the beautiful girl in the fairy-tale who could never open her mouth without letting out toads, vipers, and other ugly creatures.

Author Unknown
The Bazar Book of Decorum (1870) 138

Volume

She should by all means avoid an affected tone of voice – neither speaking too loud nor yet too low. The former may bring on her the accusation of rudeness; the latter subject her to the charge of whispering – which is at all times an invidious thing.

A Lady of New York
Etiquette for Ladies (1843) 38-39

Some persons appear to go to the very extreme, and deafen you; they may speak the words of wisdom, but you wish them dumb. Others mumble so that you are forced continually to express your total inability to follow the drift of their remarks; others drawl so that you feel that life is not long enough for such acquaintance.

Henry Davenport Northrop
The Household Encyclopedia (189?) 23

Vocal Tone

There are women, beautiful of feature and form, graceful of carriage, who yet have few or no admirers, because, when they speak, the charm is dispelled by a harsh, disagreeable voice. On the other hand, a commonplace little woman, to all appearances, may possess powers of fascination almost unlimited because of the low, sweet melody that pours from her lips, soothing to the wearied one, a tonic to the ill and sorrowing, sweetest music to husband and children and an uplifting power to all who come within its sound.

Alice M. Long
My Lady Beautiful (1906) 173-174

The quality of tone in the voice deserves the most careful attention of young people who desire to possess the best acquirements of culture. The nasal tone, the scolding tone, the whine, the pathetic, the wheedling, the yammering, the fawning tone — all may be heard in any assemblage where people speak freely. No department is so neglected in our schools and none so imperatively needs attention as this of conversational voice culture.

Helen Ekin Starrett
The Charm of Fine Manners (1920) 115

One of the most deplorable things with many women is their utter blindness to the power residing in the quality of their voices.

Hartland and Herbert Law
Viavi Hygiene (1902) 117

Let your voice rise on the final word — not drop and swallow it. This takes practice... Practice sentences both ways. Your old way of dropping your voice; the new way of raising your voice ever so slightly as if every sentence were a question.

Rebecca
How to be The Smart Woman (1946) 55

Whisper the word, "hush" again and again slowly and distinctly. Then repeat several times in the same manner these sentences: "Softly, softly whisper the words of love. Silence is over all. The night is hushed and still." Again repeat the same in a low and quiet undertone. Now repeat several times in the purest, tenderest voice that you can command, "I shall speak softly and sweetly today beautiful words of love. Pearls and diamonds of speech only shall issue from my lips. Sweet, pure tones shall make me better and they shall be as music to my friends and loved ones."

Alice M. Long
My Lady Beautiful (1906) 179-180

Conversation

A great help in keeping a general conversation on a pleasant level of congeniality is to see that it does not move from the drawing room to the stable, hospital or boudoir. Especially at dinner, topics horsily flavored, that bring a whiff of the antiseptics of the operating table, which air the details of personal ills or personal blemishes, the impedimenta and practices of the dressing room, are neither congenial nor fit subjects for discussion.. And this applies as well to the personal joke, always in bad form.

... And in her conversation tact is of the utmost importance. She will not relate to an old bachelor sitting next to her every cunning little trick baby performs. She will not extol her husband's many fine qualities to a young man of her own age. She avoids arguments and flat contradictions. She will not talk to old folks about the disadvantages of age, nor praise dancing to the lame....

Harriet Lane
The Book of Culture (1922) 45, 29

A young lady should remember that silence is golden, and not speak too often, or too long, or too glibly.

Author Unknown
The Standard Book on Politeness (1884) 79

To begin a story or narration, when you are not perfect in it, and cannot go through with it, but are forced, possibly, to say in the middle of it, "I have forgot the rest," is very unpleasant and bungling.

Utley E. Crane, Ed.
New Outline of Knowledge, Vol. X (1936) 477

Do not forget names, nor mistake one name for another. To speak of Mr. What-d'ye-call-him, or You-know-who, Mrs. Thingum, What's-her-name, or How-d'ye-call-her, is exceedingly coarse and unladylike."

Emily Thornwell
The Lady's Guide to Perfect Gentility (1856) 153

Gesticulate as little as you can while speaking. Do not spread out your fingers like a fan, nor point them at your neighbor like so many darts.

Frances Smith
Talks with Homely Girls (1885) 145-146

Vocabulary

void affectations. In conversation make use of long words as little as possible, and wherever a short and easily understood one is suitable to express your meaning, choose it in preference to one of polysyllabic proportions.

Maud C. Cooke
Manual of Social Forms (1896) 174

n conversation, one must scrupulously guard against vulgarisms. Simplicity and terseness of language are the characteristics of a well educated and highly cultivated person. It is the uneducated or those who are but half educated, who use long words and high-sounding phrases. A hyperbolical way of speaking is mere flippancy, and should be avoided. Such phrases as "awfully pretty," "immensely jolly," "abominably stupid," "disgustingly mean," are of this nature, and should be avoided. Awkwardness of attitude is equally as bad as awkwardness of speech. Lolling, gesticulating, fidgeting, handling an eye-glass or watch chain and the like, give an air of *gaucherie*, and take off a certain percentage from the respect of others.

John H. Young
Our Deportment (1880) 87

on't say elegant to mean everything that pleases you.

Don't say genteel for well-bred.

Don't say she does not see any; say she does not see at all.

Don't say he calculates to get off; say he expects to get off.

Don't say where are you stopping? say where are you staying?

Don't say party for person.

Don't use slangy words; they are vulgar.

Don't use profane words; they are sinful and foolish.

Don't say lit the fire; say lighted the fire.

Don't say if I am not mistaken you are in the wrong; say if I mistake not.

Don't say I bought a new pair of shoes; say I bought a pair of new shoes.

B.G. Jefferis and J.L. Nichols
Search Lights on Health (1902) 57-58

DO NOT SAY: – "PLEASED TO MEET YOU." Probably you are "pleased" to meet your new acquaintance, but people with good manners simply do not use those words. They consider this response the worst that could possibly be made.

Author Unknown
Good Manners (1930) 15

The word "ma'am" for "madam," in polite use many years ago, is no longer a part of the vocabulary of even a child.

Adults do not say "Yes, ma'am" and "No, ma'am." Perhaps the ash collector might use these expressions to a woman from whose home he carries ashes. Not knowing her name, and thinking the curt "yes" or "no" impolite, he would say "ma'am." Maybe the delivery boy of little or no training would do the same.

"Ma'am" stamps you as a country bumpkin or a mental and social inferior. You might as well say, "I am inferior to you. It is nice of you to talk to me; so I'll be very polite."...

Over the telephone "ma'am" gives the person to whom it is used a very poor opinion of the education of the one who uses it.

Don't forget that your morals may be the finest, your heart as kind as another's, your appearance all that is to be desired, but say "ma'am" over the telephone to an educated person and you will not be on his list.

To make the point very clear, just visualize this situation:

Miss Trent, the high-school teacher, has taught

her English pupils never to say "Yes, ma'am." She is absent from home one evening when the head of her department calls her.

Head of department: *"Is Miss Trent at home?"*

Mother: *"No, ma'am."*

Head of department: *"Do you know when she will return?"*

Mother: *"No, ma'am."*

The next day at school the principal, an admirer of Miss Trent, says: *"Miss Trent's family must be charming people. Have you met them?"*

Head of department (sneeringly): *"Yes. The mother says 'ma'am'."*

Sophia C. Hadida
Manners for Millions (1935) 120-121

Slang and Colloquialisms Which Will Not Pass Muster

Aggravating Papa	A refractory lover
Ball up	Confuse, mix
Big bug	A person of prominence
Cake-eater	Effeminate young man
Chew the rag	Wrangle; talk
Cluck	A silly, foolish person
Cuckoo	Intoxicated

Finale hopper	A dancing man who always stays to the last dance
Frail	A girl
Full	Intoxicated
Geezer	A disrespectful phrase applied to elderly persons
Get a gait on	Hasten or hurry
Grass widow	A woman living separate from her husband
Gum the works	Spoil anything through a blunder
Heavy-sugar papa	An elderly lover
Poor fish	A person who cannot be taken seriously or is to be pitied
Jag (jagged)	Drunk
Jazz baby	A frivolous young woman
Jazz hound	A young society idler
Jaw (jawing)	Talk
Lit-up	Intoxicated
Lounge lizard	(See: Cake eater)
Nifty; nobby	Stylish, showy
Paste	To hit
Peel (to)	Disrobe
Perfectly killing	Very stylishly
Pie-eyed	Intoxicated

Piker	A cheap, small-minded person
Pile-in	Get to work
Pipe-off	Take in at a single glance
Prune	A tiresome or uninteresting person
Push	All those forming a party
Rag	To tease
Skunk	An altogether objectionable character
Screw loose	Mentally not quite responsible
Soused	Intoxicated
Spiffilicated	Intoxicated
Stew bum	Habitual drunkard and loafer
Tickle the tusks	Play the piano
Tie the bull	Stop bluffing or talking nonsense
Togged out	Well-dressed
Wild woman	An objectionable euphemism for a girl or woman who is no better than she should be
Yappy	Foolish

Utley E. Crane
New Outline of Knowledge, Vol. X (1936) 146-152

Pronunciation

There are some persons who spray when they talk. This is very annoying to their associates. Friends speak about the necessity for carrying an umbrella when around Mary. Mary knows that she has this affliction, but it has never occurred to her to cure herself.

To obviate this difficulty all Mary would have to do would be to talk more slowly and be very careful when saying words that begin with the letters b and p and perhaps with a, c, d, e, f, g, h, i, j, k, l, m, n, o, q, r, s, t, u, v, w, x, y, and z. With those exceptions she could speak with ease and give no thought to the showers.

Sophia C. Hadida
Manners for Millions (1935) 64

As Sometimes Said:	Preferable:
Noo (new)	nyew
ex-*quis*-ite	*ex*-quisite
ak-kli-*mate*-ed (acclimated)	Ak-*klime*-ated
nef-few (nephew)	Nev-vew

Margery Wilson
The Pocket Book of Etiquette (1940) 153-154

Profanity

Such exclamations as "Not Much," or "Heavens," or "Good Gracious," should never be used. If you are surprised or astonished, suppress the fact. Such expressions border closely on profanity.

Georgene Corry Benham
Polite Life and Etiquette (1902) 105-106

No lady should make use of any feminine substitute for profanity. The woman who exclaims "The dickens!" or "Mercy!" or "Goodness!" when she is annoyed or astonished, is as vulgar in spirit, though perhaps not quite so regarded by society, as though she had used expressions which it would require but little stretch of the imagination to be regarded as profane.

John H. Young
Our Deportment (1880) 98

Eliminate such profane words as "damn" and "hell" from your vocabulary. They do not add charm to your personality.

Sophia C. Hadida
Manners for Millions (1935) 72

When one hears an indelicate word or expression...not the shadow of a smile should flit across the lips. Either complete silence should be preserved in return or the words, "I do not understand you," be spoken. A lady will always fail to hear that which she should not hear, or, having unmistakably heard, she will not understand.

Author Unknown
Social Culture (1902) 59

Thoughtless, brazen, painted, cigarette-smoking, cocktail-drinking women are not likely to think and speak purely...

Young girls need to be on guard against older women who are purveyors of filthy talk.

Clayton Derstine
Paths to Beautiful Womanhood (1944) 42

Physique

" A woman can never be too rich or too insecure about her weight." That's the way the old maxim ought to go.

Women's bodies have long been treated as a fashion item, and the styles have changed repeatedly, in cycles, over the decades. Plump, thin; large-breasted, small-breasted; indulgently languid, rigidly exercised – such fickle fluxes and contradictions are found in these pages.

One theory has it that the body-fashion becomes thin and small-breasted in eras when women are gaining power, such as the 1920s and the 1970s, while rounded, womanly figures are popular when women are urged to stay home and lifestyle choices are more limited – typified in the wasp-waisted, pointed breasts of the 1950s.

Perhaps that explains the now-fashionable "not found in nature" body ideal of today. In an era pushing women to do it all, we idolize an impossible image: Amazon tall, size 2, with DD breasts.

Thanks a lot Barbie, we might say. But the image isn't entirely new – only the surgery that makes it possible. Herein you'll find a 1905 formula for the perfect female body, recommending 138 pounds and a 24" waist. Go figure.

You'll also find wistful remembrances of a time when "massive hips" were prized, descriptions of weird exercises (be sure the blinds are drawn), and rather masochistic methods from that dominatrix of the deco era, Sylvia of Hollywood.

And, in case body-fashion changes again in our lifetimes, you'll find what looks like a messy, smelly, and skin-stinging method of breast reduction.

With so much cultural scrutiny of our bodies, it's no wonder women have become obsessed with physical self-criticism. It's time to retire the notion of fashion in physiques. In the meantime, we could always hide under mu-mus. They're so much prettier than burkas.

Ugliness is a Sin

Ugliness is a sin, sometimes of the worst character. The victim of physical defects in appearance is not in all cases the sinner. She may have been sinned against previous to her birth by several generations. She may have inherited the defects displayed by features and form, and under such circumstances she cannot always be blamed.

In spite of one's inheritance, however, there is absolutely no excuse for one being so extremely unattractive as to be ugly. From this standpoint ugliness is truly sinful and the sin is committed almost entirely by the victim herself. Her sinfulness may have been caused largely by ignorance, but that excuse in no way interferes with the results. If one does not take proper care of the body, the marks of this neglect will be very plainly emphasized. If one fails to develop the body as one grows from girlhood to womanhood, it will usually be weak, poorly formed and unattractive in appearance.

My dear reader, if you are what is termed "ugly," you may be able to blame your parents for neglecting to give you information of yourself about which you should have been fully informed, but beyond this you will be personally responsible....

NO WOMAN HAS ANY BUSINESS TO BE UGLY. It is sinful to bring about such deplorable physical results, and it is still more sinful to allow physical defects of this kind to remain.

Bernarr Macfadden
"Ugliness is a Sin"
Beauty and Health Vol . XIII (1908) 34

 beautiful woman is more beautiful than any other beautiful thing in the world.

Hartland and Herbert Law
Viavi Hygiene (1902) 107

Thinness

If there are some persons who are anxious to get rid of fat, there are many more, particularly in our country, who are desirous of acquiring it.

Author Unknown
The Bazar Book of Decorum (1870) 86

Most thin women want to put on weight, be "just a little heavier and fuller." They cannot be blamed for this: when the thin woman acquires just that little extra fullness she becomes sylph-like, and good clothes look better on her. She herself looks better and feels better. And so it is the urge to beauty that drives the thin woman, and she will move the immovable to satisfy this urge.

J. Howard Crum
The Truth About Beauty (1933) 56

If young girls don't stop reducing when their present figures are at the point of emaciation, I'm going to call a mass meeting and spank every one of these youngsters!

Thin Women!! Gain!!
Three to five pounds a week

Youthful, Round Cheeks—Plump Snowy Neck—Full, Dainty, Womanly Development —Adorably Plump Body—Guaranteed Yours.

Beautiful, Firm, Permanent Flesh Produced. Healthfully and Rapidly. No Medicine, No Exercise. Physicians Themselves Write for Help.

In Writing, Please Enclose 2 Cent Stamp. *I Hope to Hear from You.*

The Star Developing System   Iron Mountain Michigan

In the first place (and this is rather more important to the present generation than health) scrawny figures have definitely gone out of fashion.

First, scientists berated us because we were so skinny, throwing the fear of ill health into us if we continued the drastic reducing measures necessary to attain the angles so favored during the past few years. And then Fashion nodded her fastidious head in accord with science by favoring the new curved mode.

I don't mean that we are entering an era of hips and chests, but I do mean that Fashion has swung her whimsical pendulum from excessive thinness to pleasing roundness and, as one famous fashion creator said, "It's about time, for I'm tired of trying to fit beautiful silks and satins to a rack of skin and bones!"

Josephine Huddleston
Secrets of Charm (1929) 113

To render the waist small, large hips are a natural necessity.

Dr. A. Cazenave
Beauty (1877) 94

If you are painfully thin in particular places, as on your upper arms, your thighs, your knees and elbows, your neck, your cheeks, a daily massage of these parts with lanolin or cocoa butter, patting in all that the parts can absorb, will fill them out in no time — only persist in it.

But there is no reason why one should try to achieve a matchlike slenderness. Like all perverted fashion ideas, the craze for matchlike slenderness has come and gone.

Dare Frances
Lovely Ladies: The Art of Being a Woman (1929) 277-278; 266-267

Plumpness

It's a Sin To Stay Fat

So Easy to Reduce

Look about you. Note how slender figures now displace the fat so common years ago. There has come a new era, based on a new discovery. Doctors the world over now employ it. The results are seen in every circle.

When you know how fat blights health, beauty and efficiency—how it robs life of half its joys—don't you think it a sin to stay fat?

Some years ago, medical research discovered a great cause of excess fat. It lies in a weakened gland, whose secretions largely control nutrition. That gland secretion is intended to change food into fuel and energy. If it is scant, too much food turns to fat.

Since that discovery, doctors the world over have been feeding that gland in obesity. The results have brought a new era to the over-fat, as you see on every side.

Marmola prescription tablets are based on that gland factor which modern doctors now employ. The tablets are employed by a world-famous medical laboratory. They have been used for 24 years—millions of boxes of them. Most of you have friends who can tell you what they do.

Wise people have deserted the old ways of reduction—abnormal exercise and diet, harmful drugs. And the false treatments, of which there have been so many. They are keeping slender in this easy, pleasant, right way. And they are gaining new health and vitality as the weight goes down.

Each box of Marmola contains the formula complete. Also a complete explanation as to why the pounds go. You know exactly what you are taking, and why.

Go get a box today. Price $1.00. It is folly to stay fat in these scientific days. Simply take four tablets daily until weight comes down to normal.

MARMOLA
PRESCRIPTION TABLETS
The Right Way to Reduce

You've all heard the old saying, "The way to a man's heart is through his stomach." Well, let me tell you, the looks of *yours* has a lot to do with winning his heart.

Sylvia of Hollywood
Streamline Your Figure (1939) 26

Any stubborn lump of flesh can be squeezed off... It works perfectly on all parts of the body, hips, thighs, waist, anywhere in fact except the breasts. Never squeeze or massage the breasts.

First, cover your hands with massaging cream. Take up handfuls of flesh, squeeze hard, then let it slip through your fingers like mashed potatoes. You can squeeze off fat cells in this manner exactly like I worked on the stars with my hands. After squeezing, put a Turkish towel over the part you're reducing and slap good and hard.

Sylvia of Hollywood
No More Alibis! (1934) 45

ccording to a computation made as to what the perfect symmetrical figure of a woman of 5ft. 5in. in height should be, the following is the standard: — She should be 138 lbs. in weight (but an additional 10 lbs. will be no detriment to her perfect proportion); her bust should be 43 inches, measured over the arms, and her waist 24 inches; the upper part of the arm should be from 13-1/2 to 14 inches, and the wrist 6 inches; the ankle should be 6 inches, the calf of the leg 14 inches, and the thigh 20 inches.

Boyd Laynard
Secrets of Beauty, Health and Long Life (1905) 36-37

Breasts

It is a sad fact that women suffering from pendulous breasts are often among the most fastidious of their sex. Martyrs to unsightly bust development frequently feel their affliction keenly, and this vivid realization interferes with their attainment of the serene mood necessary for the execution of work or the enjoyment of recreation....

A sloppy and distressing protuberance is today

easily changed for the classic appeal of a firm-bosomed statue. A full-busted woman of taste can now become as refined a conception of beauty as her artistically planned wardrobe...

An investigation of countless operations on pendulous breasts reveals the fact that these corrections are quite harmless, and, indeed, are actually beneficial from a health point of view. It stands to reason that any woman is better off without a heavy load of flesh lying on her heart and muscles and interfering with all comfortable as well as graceful athletic movements.

J. Howard Crum
The Truth About Beauty (1933) 190-191

Wear a brassiere that properly supports you, otherwise your neck and face muscles will sag.

Monsieur Georges A. Sakele
One Thousand and One Beauty Hints (1931) 11

To reduce the bust stand straight, hands on hips. Move the elbows back till they meet. Then, stretching out your arms in front of you, the palms of the hands meeting, raise the arms above the head, again stretch them out, and return, slowly.

Florence Courtenay
Physical Beauty (1922) 19

The chest should be large, well raised, and gracefully rounded. To be well-placed, the breasts should have an interval between, equal to that which exists between the nipples and the middle of the hollow of the collar-bones. They should be slightly rounded, little, hard, and not too much attached to the body.

Dr. A. Cazenave
Beauty (1877) 93

"Glory, I am reducing all over very rapidly, but my bust still seems so prominent, and I do hate to wear such tight brassieres, as I must to have a boyish form. Would it be too much of a miracle for you to help me reduce that particular spot?" This plea from Rose to Glory one morning after her reduction bath.

"No, indeed, Rose, I can help you reduce — I had to myself for I ran altogether too much to those curves... I'll tell you what I did. I took two pounds of epsom salts and poured over them one gallon of boiling water and put it in a granite saucepan with a cover, so I could just let it stay there between treatments.

"I kept one large Turkish towel just for this purpose; and every day I heated the salts, wet the towel with them and laid it over the bust, covering it with a piece of rubberized cloth to keep in the heat as long as possible and prevent everything from getting damp. I did this for half an hour on a stretch, and then finished by bathing in warm water and rubbing on the same lotion that I will have made up for you.

"... The lotion is easy to make. Take two ounces of gum camphor and dissolve in a pint of witch hazel or pure alcohol, if you can get it. Dissolve one pound of epsom salts in one pint of boiling water

and pour in one ounce of colorless iodine and com-
bine the two mixtures. Rub on the bust or any other
particularly fat place twice a day. The results are
amazing."

Mabelle A. Burbridge
The Road to Beauty (1924) 124-126

Exercise

There can be no grace without elasticity. Elasticity is the secret of beauty. You want elastic limbs, elastic flesh, elastic muscles, elastic nerves, elastic brains, elastic manners, in fact, elastic everything, except elastic morals....

Excessive exercise makes a woman all knees, elbows, and knuckle-joints. Violent athletics coarsen the bones and give unlovely prominence to distinctive parts and muscles. The form of a youthful woman should have the lineaments and agile grace of a wood-nymph — slight and elastic in all her parts, her limbs moving in harmony with nature's tapering curves. With this picture in view, it will be seen that the efforts required for lawn-tennis and similar diversions would be rather vehement for the average woman...

Annie Wolf
The Truth About Beauty (1892) 47, 59-60

Now we jump out of bed and chop wood! It is a wonderful exercise for almost every part of the body, which must have a certain amount of exercise in order to function properly. Stand with your legs apart and your arms straight up and clasped high over your head, as though you were holding a hatchet. Then, whang goes the hatchet down between your feet! It's a very short hatchet, and you give it such a blow that the log of wood cracks right in two and flies across the room. But there are more logs, so you cut up six or eight every morning...

Dare Frances
Lovely Ladies: The Art of Being a Woman (1929) 255

The piano, that family vampire, has sapped the vitality of thousands of young girls, by keeping them from the healthful recreation and exercise which they so much need.

Frances Smith
Talks with Homely Girls (1886) 38

Many people dislike back-bending exercises, or those in which stooping or bending to the floor plays a considerable part. With these people we are in full sympathy; nothing would make us give up a routine more quickly. In fact, bending exercises of any kind frequently produce dizziness and other unpleasant symptoms. All these objectionable features are entirely avoided in the exercise that we have called the "Charleston Twist."

... Simply jump up in the air and land on the left foot; as you land on the left foot you throw the right leg straight out — sideways — and turn the foot in toward the body as far as you can. Repeat by jumping on the right foot and throwing the left leg out. This exercise should be done in your bedroom where you can do it in the nude before a mirror. Thus you can observe the movements of the muscles... No brassiere should be worn during this exercise; by allowing full play to the breast you will note a gradual firming and molding that is really remarkable.

The Twist should be done rapidly, and the jump into the air as high as possible. It is especially important that the leg and foot be turned in toward the body as far as possible. If considerable effort is put into this exercise, the benefits to be derived are really wonderful, for it calls into play practically every muscle in the body, below the neck...

The Charleston Twist will also have a tendency to firm the cheeks if the mouth is kept open during the exercise...

... Rain or shine, come what may, the Charleston Twist must go on twice daily.

J. Howard Crum
The Truth About Beauty (1933) 35-38

Suspend a ball from the ceiling, chandelier or doorway, and holding the arms at right angles with the body, strike it first with one elbow and then the other with an upward movement. Continue this until slightly fatigued.

Alice M. Long
My Lady Beautiful (1906) 166

Squat down with knees spread out sideways, heels together and hands on the floor in front of you. Without moving your hands, take a quick jump and throw the feet apart about eighteen inches. Now hop back to starting position with heels together. Repeat hoppings ten to twenty times.

Lois Leeds and Hilda M. Kaji
Beauty and Health (1927) 244

Sit on the floor, stomach pulled in, *coda* tucked under. Lean back slightly, propping yourself with your arms. Now bump on the plump of your bustle. Bump and bump and bump, twice for each year of your age.

Rebecca
How to be The Smart Woman (1946) 62

With body in position as above bend forward far to the right, change position of legs, then same exercise to the left.

Bernarr Macfadden
The Power and Beauty of Superb Womanhood (1901) 161

Pleasing Men

Good Female Body. — No weakly, poor-bodied woman can draw a man's love like a strong, well developed body. A round, plump figure with an overflow of animal life is the woman most commonly sought...

Broad Hips. — A woman with a large pelvis gives her a superior and significant appearance, while a narrow pelvis always indicate(s) weak sexuality...

Full Busts. — In the female beauty of physical development there is nothing that can equal full breasts. It is an indication of good health and good maternal qualities. As a face looks bad without a nose, so the female breast, when narrow and flat, produces a bad effect... As woman looks so much better with artificial paddings and puffings than she does without, therefore modern society should waive all objections to their use....

B.G. Jefferis and J.L. Nichols
Search Lights on Health (1902) 130

Man admires voluptuous plumpness in woman, a smooth and fair skin, an oval face, full and round arms, good breasts, massive hips and thighs...

C.S. Whitehead and Charles A. Hoff
The New Eugenics (1932) 85

If you are married, it is a clever precaution to let your husband decide what you shall weigh.

Monsieur Georges A. Sakele
One Thousand and One Beauty Hints (1931) 14

You Can Weigh
What
You Should Weigh

You can, *I know* it, because I have **reduced** 25,000 women and have **built** up as many more — scientifically, naturally, without drugs, in the privacy of their own rooms; I can build up your vitality — at the same time I strengthen your heart action; can teach you how to breathe, to stand, walk and correct such ailments as ***nervousness, torpid liver, constipation, indigestion, etc.***

One pupil writes: "I weigh 83 pounds less, and I have gained wonderfully in strength." Another says: "Last May I weighed 106 pounds, this May I weigh 126, and oh! I feel SO WELL." Write to-day for my free booklet.

SUSANNA COCROFT, Dept. 50, 624 Michigan Bl., Chicago, Ill.
Author of "Growth in Silence," "Self-Sufficiency," etc.

Appendages

Yesterday's experts criticized and advised women on various body parts with such specificity that the parts in question merit a whole chapter to themselves.

Some appendages were considered symbols of financial success, particularly the hands. The smooth, perfectly-groomed hand denoted a life of leisure rather than labor. And the fashion for ultra-white skin, while blatantly racist, also bespoke a luxurious indoor, un-sunned lifestyle, free from fields and farm work.

There's clearly a profit motive in keeping women insecure about our hands, feet, arms, legs, skin, hair — every part of our bodies from head to toe. When we're concerned about a defect, we're quite willing to open our purses to purchase a cure.

But perhaps such critical standards and insecurities originated from an entirely different motive. At a time when society's structure depended on women's dependence on men, it was threatened by the notion of ambitious, financially self-sufficient women.

How to keep them busy and challenged in the home? One way was to increase standards for home cleanliness, and burgeoning industries met and furthered the cause with new cleaning products and electrical appliances. Another, perhaps, was to keep women focused on themselves, changing and tightening standards of beauty until every minute detail of their bodies was scrutinized — even the backs of their necks!

When a woman's best chances for survival, let alone comfort, were found in marriage, it made more practical sense for her to spend hours beautifying her elbows than improving her mind.

Industry profited from, and in turn propelled, women's self-scrutiny. That may not have changed, but the specific advice and remedies certainly have.

Reading some of these tips is enough to make you bite those perfectly manicured nails. (Maybe that explains why gloves were in such fashion!)

Hands

There are many different exercises for relaxing the muscles of the hand; but I have seen the most wonderful results accomplished by merely shaking the wrists backward and forward; slowly at first, and increasing the impetus of the movement until the hands are entirely under the control of this wrist force; falling apparently lifeless upon cessation of the movement, the hand is ready for its first lesson in vital grace. With the hand and wrist perfectly passive, raise the arm at full length upward, with the hand falling naturally from the wrist in its relaxed condition. At a point above the head, when the arm is fully extended, begin the downward movement, introducing life at the wrist, and gradually into the entire hand, by depressing the wrist...

A broad, thick, short-fingered hand, of the "dumpy" variety, may be greatly improved by exercises which give mental expression and muscular flexibility. Such hands, in a crude state, usually suggest stupidity and clumsiness, and belong to people of peasant origin and the hard-working class...

Annie Jenness Miller
Physical Beauty (1894) 129-133

Stretch the right arm forward as far as possible as if pointing at some distant object. Let the fingers relax, using the forefinger to point out the object. Do this 5 times with the right hand and 5 times with the left hand.

Edyth Thornton McLeod
Your Home Course to Health, Beauty, Charm (1947) 42

Wear during the night, large cloth mittens filled with wet bran or oat-meal, and tied closely at the wrist. Persons who have a great deal of house-work to do, may keep their hands soft and white by wearing bran or oat-meal mittens.

John H. Young
Our Deportment (1880) 384

Before retiring take a large pair of gloves and spread mutton tallow inside, also all over the hands. Wear the gloves all night, and wash the hands with olive oil and white castile soap the next morning.

Mrs. Jane Warren
Ladies' Own Home Cook Book (1891) 127

The following is said to be an excellent prepara-tion for making the hands white... Take as much scraped horseradish as will fill a tablespoon; pour on it half-a-pint of hot milk. Use it before washing, al-lowing it to dry on the hands before applying the wa-ter.

Maud C. Cooke
Manual of Social Forms (1896) 505

Nails

Dainty finger-tips are the index of praise-worthy mental habits; and since the manicure has become so popular a feature of refined life, there is no excuse for grimy, ragged, and repulsive finger-ends... Trimming the nails to talon-like points and staining them tomato-color is a gross pretension and none but very vulgar women or silly girls are guilty of it.

Annie Wolf
The Truth About Beauty (1892) 84-85

Nothing is so repulsive as to see a lady or gentleman, however well dressed they may otherwise be, with nails dressed in mourning.

Richard A. Wells
Manners, Culture and Dress (1891) 380

The nail should be pared and filed to curve from side to side, and it should never be allowed to extend beyond the tip of the finger further than is necessary as an actual protection of the finger itself: more than this is suggestive of a talon or claw, or of the practices of certain pagan fanatics, who, for one reason and another, allow the nails to grow to abnormal and disgusting lengths.

Annie Jenness Miller
Physical Beauty (1894) 137-138

The only real cure for nail biting is not to bite the nails.

Florence Courtenay
Physical Beauty (1922) 48

The fanciful shapes of nails so much in vogue a few years ago have, fortunately, gone out of fashion.

Incorrect Shapes of Nails

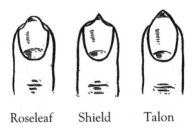

Roseleaf   Shield   Talon

William A. Woodbury
Beauty Culture (1911) 37-38

Fingers

The not uncommon practice of snapping the fingers, as it is termed, is fatal to their good looks. It stretches and weakens the ligaments, and so enlarges the knuckles and joints that the whole hand becomes knotty and of a very unsightly appearance.

Author Unknown
The Bazar Book of Decorum (1870) 64

Arms

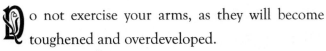

Do not exercise your arms, as they will become toughened and overdeveloped.

Monsieur Georges A. Sakele
One Thousand and One Beauty Hints (1931) 19

The beautiful arm looks as though it were made for ornament, not for use. No muscle is unduly prominent....

Try to rid the elbows of their disfiguring redness or darker color. Rub them every night before retiring with a half grape fruit. This is better than a lemon because the elbow can settle into it and work about it. If you place the halves of grape fruit on a table and rest your elbows in them you can read or chat or meditate and leave the elbows to their bleaching for an indefinite time...

An ingenious girl I know bound slices of lemon on her elbows every night before going to bed.

Mme. Lina Cavalieri
My Secrets of Beauty (1914) 69, 72

Washing especially is a good exercise if one would have beautifully rounded arms; but it is an exercise that should be taken in moderation.

Mary Ries Melendy
Vivilore (1904)161

Feet

 flat foot is an ugly foot... the intricate bridge of the foot was demolished, leaving in its wake a flat member.

... In the severe cases, the only cure seems to be through surgery, and even this may fail if the condition has been neglected for too long a time. All flat feet require medical attention and guidance.

J. Howard Crum
The Truth About Beauty (1933) 312-313

on't wear old shoes about the house. They will make your feet shapeless.

Florence Courtenay
Physical Beauty (1922) 49

ut pencils or large kindergarten crayons on the floor and as you tiptoe, dressing, whenever you come to one, pause to try to pick it up with the toes of first one foot and then the other. Give it up before it makes you nervous.

Rebecca
How to be The Smart Woman (1946) 80

The unusual arched instep, the deep hollow, the rounded ball, are marks of thorough breeding, but a pinched foot bespeaks an imbecile mind.

Annie Wolf
The Truth About Beauty (1892) 85-86

Feet and popularity are close relations. If you don't believe it, remember the dance when you had a painful corn; the tea when your shoes pinched; the hike with a gay companion, when there was a blister on your heel; the dinner party when the satin slippers began to cut across your instep.

Your face can't look serene, your conversation can't be bright, your personality can't radiate, if your feet hurt. The worst of it is that the hurt need not be acute. Even the most minor foot discomfort can erase charm and add years.

Alice Thompson and Helen Valentine
Better Than Beauty: A Guide to Charm (1938) 18

To this I willingly agree — there is nothing in the world so ugly — I will use the word to ignoble — as a pair of large flat feet; above all, when they belong to a fat person, shod in prunella, it is horrible — enough to make the dogs in the street growl...

It is more shameful for a pretty woman to have a corn or bunion on her foot, than to deceive, without a good motive, her dearest lover.

Ernest Feydeau
The Art of Pleasing (1877) 17, 23-24

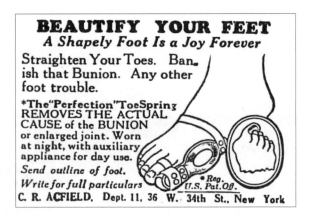

Legs

Let me whisper to the great majority of misguided women that there is no value in bulky calves. They afford the possessor absolutely nothing but a clumsy carriage. I have heard women exulting at their hugely developed calves. I have known women to pit the dimensions of their calves, one against another, as an evidence of health and a natural charm. And whenever it has been my evil fortune to pass through this experience, I have been forcibly reminded of the boy who boasted of the magnificent attachment of a mortgage to his father's property.

Annie Wolf
The Truth About Beauty (1892) 62-63

The thighs are principally remarkable among women for their fullness, the beauty of their outlines, and their polish. They should be firm, massive, and slightly touch each other above the knees.

Dr. A. Cazenave
Beauty (1877) 114

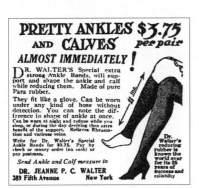

Back of the Neck

The back of the neck is usually the one place that you forget to keep well groomed! You keep it clean, and usually well shingled, if you have short hair, but it never seems to occur to even the most lovely ladies that it requires more attention than that.

Give yourself a ruthless five minutes with a couple of mirrors, and study the back of your neck. Is it pretty? Or is it long and prickly looking? Does it curve unbecomingly? Don't leave all this to everyone to see when you can just as easily select hats, collars, and scarfs that will make it attractive, or, at least, will not expose it so mercilessly to the public gaze.

Look the back of your head and neck squarely in the face, just once!

Dare Frances
Lovely Ladies: The Art of Being a Woman (1929) 197

Hygiene

Nothing could make you more grateful for modern soap, deodorant, and toothpaste than considering the alternatives: watermelon, ammonia, and charcoal.

After reading this chapter, you'll never take that morning shower for granted again! Even into the 20th century, many middle class homes didn't have indoor plumbing. Bathing was an ordeal, and a relatively infrequent one. Yet body odors didn't go unnoticed.

Hygiene wasn't always what it is today. Government funds were once devoted to educating people on its importance, in an effort to secure public health and limit disease. Scan any source of used books, and you're likely to find early 20th-century textbooks for children on hygiene. Today, if a teacher found it necessary to tell your child to bathe, you'd be called in for a "special conference."

How could a woman of the past spend so much time on her manners, speech, and every aspect of her physique right down to the back of her neck, yet still have a problem with odors?

Perhaps one explanation may be found in the rest of this book — horseradish hand soaks, camphor breast treatments, and onion hair applications, for example, not to mention the sweat-inducing "Charleston Twist" exercise.

More likely, the infrequency of baths was the problem, and it had to be a problem for both sexes. While the admonishments were written mostly to women warning that odors repel men, it's hard to assume that most men of their day smelled like roses, either.

No wonder women carried fans.

Dental hygiene was another matter. The very notion of brushing with soot, ashes, and cuttlefish will make you grateful enough to kiss your dentist, no matter how sadistic with the drill.

Just be sure you're ammonia-fresh first.

Body Odors

C leanliness of the Person. — Dr. Galopin remarks that "Love begins at the nose." An unpleasant odor always shows itself about the person of those who neglect the bath. Bad smells lead to aversion. Bad smelling persons are exceedingly disagreeable companions.

T.W. Shannon
Eugenics (1919) 63

B ut, unfortunately, with certain individuals whose hygienic conditions are perfect, and whose habits of cleanliness are minute, the odor is often most disagreeable, especially disgusting with red-haired persons and blondes.

Dr. A. Cazenave
Beauty (1877) 147

B ody odors cannot be eliminated by the use of scent. In fact, there is nothing more unpleasant than the combination of perfume and body odors. A truly dainty woman understands perfectly that it is not enough merely to bathe a great deal. One has body odors, and often very unpleasant ones, that a bath an hour could not correct but that could be corrected by some inner personal hygiene.

Dare Frances
Lovely Ladies: The Art of Being a Woman, Vol. I (1929) 303

M en are always aware of those objectionable qualities which rob woman of her charm and loveliness, but they don't tell her! The usual thing is to gradually withdraw from the woman's company, and seek companionship elsewhere. "Your best friend won't tell you," is only too true of such delicate matters as bad odors, for instance. Friends and husbands won't tell because they hesitate to hurt those they care for, and as for strangers, they are not interested. So how is one to know? These are things which the individual must find out for herself. First of all, odors should be avoided at all costs!

Leona W. Chalmers
The Intimate Side of a Woman's Life (1937) 113

B .O. has been the cause of rupture of friendships, of the breaking of engagements, of exclusion from definite social groups, of disgusted expression of the face, of quarrels between husbands and wives, friends, brothers and sisters ...

..."Birds of a feather flock together." Please notice the truth of this. You will observe that a girl guilty of B.O. has for her friends the same type... The dainty girl will have nothing to do with the one who takes a bath only on Saturday night. All the Saturday-nighters have B.O. in common, so one is not objectionable to the other.

Sophia C. Hadida
Manners for Millions (1935) 103, 265

Bathing

While it is an absolute necessity to keep clean, it is not needed to make a duck of oneself. Some people are fond of going to extremes, and there is such a thing in this direction as well as in any other. We are not aquatic animals, and therefore an excessive indulgence in the luxury of the bath weakens and enervates. I have known persons to stay a half an hour in the tub, and perhaps longer, but evil consequences are sure to follow.

Too much bathing will often bring on diseases which it is almost impossible to get rid of.

Emily S. Bouton
Health and Beauty (1884)183

While in the tub I play about as joyfully as a young porpoise. I plunge and flounder and toss up a shower of water with my hands; for to lie lazily in a tub of water is to invite rheumatism and neuralgia.

I f those who perspire freely would use a little ammonia in the water they bathe in every day, it
would keep their flesh sweet and clean, doing away
with any disagreeable odor.

Mrs. Jane Warren
Ladies' Own Home Cook Book (1891) 196

W atermelon Rub. — Rubbing the face, neck and
arms with the pulp of a watermelon has an excellent effect in clearing the skin.

Tomato Bleach. — To make a yellow skin more
clear, take a slice of a ripe tomato, rub well upon
hands, neck or shoulders for five minutes and then
rinse off with water mixed with borax.

B. Frank Scholl
Library of Health, Vol. II (1916) 1636

Breath

If you must eat odorous foods, by all means do so, but don't think merely saying, "You must excuse me because I had onions to-day," is sufficient excuse for you to go on blowing your unpleasant breath in another's face.

Dare Frances
Lovely Ladies: The Art of Being a Woman, Vol. I, (1929) 303

There are kinds of food which are uncleanly and unsafe. Onions taint the breath too much for general society. If all eat onions, it is different. Cabbage is doubtful. Some kinds of fish, as herrings, not only taint the breath, but their odor exudes from the skin.

Monfort B. Allen and Amelia C. McGregor
The Glory of Woman (1896) 451

Few things are so repellent to man as a bad odor from his partner's mouth, and this condition alone has been the cause for divorce.

William J. Robinson
Woman: Her Sex and Love Life (1938) 102

The taint of onions may be removed with parsley leaves, with vinegar or burnt coffee.

Walter R. Houghton et. al.
American Etiquette and Rules of Politeness (1884) 243

The best treatment in regard to offensive breath is the use of powdered charcoal, two or three tablespoons per week, taken in a glass of water before retiring for the night.

Mrs. Jane Warren
Ladies' Own Home Cook Book (1891) 91

Teeth

Rye contains carbonate of lime, carbonate of magnesia, oxide of iron, manganese, and silica, all suitable for application to the teeth. Therefore a fine tooth-powder is made by burning rye, or rye bread, to ashes, and grinding it to powder by passing the rolling pin over it. Pass the powder through a fine sieve and use.

Author Unknown
Decorum (1880) 334-335

Tartar can be removed by using pumice stone reduced to powder, rubbing it on the teeth with a bit of soft wood made into a brush.

Mrs. Jane Warren
Ladies' Own Home Cook Book (1891) 129

Recently-burnt charcoal, in very fine powder, is another popular and excellent tooth-powder which, without injuring the enamel, is sufficiently gritty to clean the teeth and remove the tartar from them, and possesses the advantage of also removing the offensive odor arising from rotten teeth, and from decomposing organic matter.

Monfort B. Allen and Amelia C. McGregor
The Glory of Woman (1896) 431

A good way to clean teeth is to dip the brush in water, rub it over white castile soap, then dip it in prepared chalk, and brush the teeth briskly.

John H. Young
Our Deportment (1880) 388

The best tooth-powders are made from cuttle-fish, prepared chalk, and orris-root commingled together in equal quantities.

Florence Hartley
Ladies' Book of Etiquette (1873) 312

The simplest means to preserve the teeth, is to brush them daily in a little soap and water, and magnesia.

Dr. A. Cazenave
Beauty (1877) 79

To whiten discoloured teeth, nothing can be more efficacious than using a little soot.

Boyd Laynard
Secrets of Beauty, Health and Long Life (1905) 35

The teeth need exercise just as much as the arms and legs, and this exercise can be afforded the teeth by means of a turkish towel. Push part of the turkish towel into the mouth, grip it with the teeth and give it generous jerks with both hands. This will stimulate the growth of the teeth and keep the gums radio-active.

John Hewins Kern
Glorious Womanhood (1925) 61

Hair

And you thought *you* had bad hair days!

It's often been said that every woman with curly hair wishes it were straight, and every woman with straight hair wishes it were curly. But your sisters of yesteryear probably just wished it would go away.

(And if it did, they resorted to arsenic injections.)

While we have choices — long, short, layered, dyed, permed — not so long ago, simply having short hair was considered a radical political statement. Women's hair was, for decades, as long as possible. Some of us remember the return of that fashion in the 1970s, when sitting down required lifting up our hair first.

Even today, hair styles say something about ourselves. Especially on young women, long styles still carry a message of femininity; short cuts convey an edgy stylishness. But there the similarities to past eras end.

While three days without a shampoo is disgusting now, three weeks was too often then. While we use gel and mousse, our foremothers used lard and suet. Wax is back, though.

Shampoos were made of all sorts of ingredients, from eggs to tar. (Omitted here, however, are the instructions for gasoline shampoo found in one source, as I'm rather reluctant to face baldheaded burn victims in a court of law.)

Considering our past sisters' infrequency of shampoos, strange pomades, odd styles, and bizarre color treatments, it's no wonder no self-respecting woman left home without a hat!

After reading this chapter, it's hard to look at old photographs of women without wondering whether she has onion, mutton suet, or gum-water in her hair. Perish the thought.

And please don't pass the pomade.

Cutting

It is beneficial to trim the ends of long hair once a month during the first quarter of the moon.

Monsieur Georges A. Sakele
One Thousand and One Beauty Hints (1931) 20

For a woman to persist in wearing her hair short, unless there is some special necessity for it, shows a perverted taste; woman detracts from her charm just in so far as she tries to look like a man.

Carl Rosen
The Face, Hair and Scalp (1906) 101

A woman's hair should never be cut short after the age of puberty or maturity, for in many cases it is impossible ever again to regain the full growth.

B. Frank Scholl
Library of Health, Vol. II (1916) 1639

Girls are afraid to bob their hair because pa has done some yelling and screaming on the subject. Now what can papa do, if you have your hair cut?

Sylvia of Hollywood
Pull Yourself Together, Baby! (1936) 129

Washing

How often should hair be shampooed? That is a question frequently asked and the reply is: At least once a month, and if situated in the midst of dirt, dust and all the other detriments to beauty, as is the case with many who are employed in town offices, a shampoo is necessary every two weeks.

Ellye Howell Glover
"Dame Curtsey's" Book of Beauty Talks (1923) 54

Oily hair is sometimes the result of too frequent shampooing. One tries to correct this condition by washing the scalp, which is a great mistake. If, instead, you will not wash your hair for at least six weeks, giving it a dry shampoo twice a week and a correct and persistent scalp massage two or three times a day, your hair will regain its natural health and glossiness and keep it as long as you give it the proper care.

Dare Frances
Lovely Ladies: The Art of Being a Woman, Vol. I (1929) 210-211

In general it may be stated that a monthly shampoo is quite enough for most adult heads; the exceptions are diseased conditions, and where persons are exposed to unusual dust and dirt, and must resort to water oftener... Wetting the hair daily is a great mistake for both men and women...

Annie Jenness Miller
Physical Beauty: How to Obtain and Preserve It (1894)110

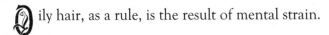

Oily hair, as a rule, is the result of mental strain.

Viola and Alexander Swan
Beauty's Question and Answer Dictionary (1931) 29

Shampoo

Egg Shampoo — Beat the whites of two eggs as stiff as possible; take all of the egg, a handful at a time, and rub it in the scalp with a light circular movement of the fingers. Dry the hair in the sun for twenty minutes; then brush it with a cleaning brush for several minutes. This leaves the hair clean and fluffy.

A. L. Fowler
Fowler's Blue Book of Selected Household Helps (1925) 61

Pure unscented salad oil is all that is required for the hair, and this should be applied with the hands, and rubbed off with flannel before going to bed, so as not to stain the pillow.

Ammonia diluted in water makes a good wash for the head...

Anonymous
Perfect Etiquette (1873?) 71

Hot Oil and Tar Shampoo
A very beneficial shampoo. Mix equal parts of hot olive-oil and tar, and rub into the scalp ten minutes before shampooing.

J. Howard Crum
The Truth About Beauty (1933) 236

Pomade

Pomade. — Two ounces of lard, two ounces of olive oil, half an ounce of rose oil, and scent to fancy.

Henry Davenport Northrop
The Household Encyclopedia (189?) 257

Take of white mutton suet 4 pounds, well boiled in hot water, (3 quarts,) and washed to free it from salt. Melt the suet, when dried, with 1 1\2 pounds of fresh lard, and 2 pounds of yellow wax. Pour into an earthen vessel, and stir till it is cold; then beat into it 30 drops of oil of cloves, or any other essential oil whose scent you prefer.

Florence Hartley
Ladies' Book of Etiquette (1873) 314

Nothing is simpler or better in the way of oil than pure, unscented salad oil, and in the way of a pomatum, bear's grease is as pleasant as anything.

John H. Young
Our Deportment (1880) 354

Hair Loss

I t would help many women grow beautiful hair if they would lift weights with their tresses. The lifting of an iron every morning would work wonders to stimulate the growth. Attach a string to an ordinary iron, fasten the string to the tresses of hair, and lift the weight five or ten times every morning and every night.

John Hewins Kern
Glorious Womanhood (1925) 63

I f women continue to bob their hair, then in time, when the demands upon the scalp muscles are lightened, the muscles will outgrow their usefulness and relax, losing their grip on the hair, and the hair will fall out...

Scalp massage is one of the finest preventive agencies against the loss of hair. But far superior to this is another simple treatment, a mild form of hair-abuse that has redeeming qualities: A daily hair-pulling treatment has no equal for strengthening the hair and the scalp-muscle connection.

J. Howard Crum
The Truth About Beauty (1933) 213

Onions must be rubbed frequently on the part. The stimulating powers of this vegetable are of essential service in restoring the tone of the skin, and assisting the capillary vessels in sending forth new hair...

Mrs. Jane Warren
Ladies' Own Home Cook Book (1891) 126

When the hair shows a tendency to fall out, the very best thing to stop its coming out and promote its growth is the abundant use of genuine olive oil. Saturate the hair thoroughly, and keep it saturated for a week, until the scalp has absorbed all it will, then wash with pure soap and water. If this operation is repeated every two or three months, the effect is said to be marvelous.

Prof. and Mrs. J. W. Gibson
Social Purity (1908) 125

If your hair persistently continues to fall out, it is probably because of a generally lowered tone of your health. I should then resort to iron or arsenic hypodermic injections under the direction of a physician.

Mme. Lina Cavalieri
My Secrets of Beauty (1914) 107

Styles

Considering the hair as a head covering, it is often most indiscreetly used. It is allowed to grow too long, and to oppress the head by its needless weight; or it is massed into knobs and protuberances, that leave one part of the scalp almost bare and another part unduly covered up; or false hair is indulged in, and collections of this material are located upon the scalp in spots indicated by fashion, with the result that undue pressure is brought to bear upon the skin, and the temperature of the head is disturbed and rendered unequal.

Monfort B. Allen and Amelia C. McGregor
The Glory of Woman (1896) 442

Do not wear a "rat" if you desire to avoid a very unsightly and unhealthy article.

Alice M. Long
My Lady Beautiful (1906) 195

Dye

French hair dye is made as follows: Melt together in a bowl set in boiling water, four ounces of white wax in nine ounces of olive oil, stirring in when melted two ounces of burnt cork in powder. To apply, put on old gloves, cover the shoulders carefully, and spread on like a pomade, brushing in well through the hair.

Walter R. Houghton et. al.
American Etiquette and Rules of Politeness (1884) 399

Should Women Dye?
"No" is the proper and logical answer to this question. Dyeing is a hair crime. In most cases it destroys the light, shade and luster of the hair, and usually — unless so subtly done as to be past detection it is a hallmark of vulgarity.

Utley E. Crane, Ed.
New Outline of Knowledge, Vol. X (1936) 379

Besides, madhouses are full of the victims of hair bleach and hair dye, as any expert on insanity will tell you.

Elizabeth Anstruther
The Complete Beauty Book (1912) 96

P aralysis of the brain has been occasioned by the inordinate use of hair dyes...

John Coulter
The New Century Perfect Speaker (1901) 546

U nder no circumstances should a woman un-dergo the treatment during menstruation, be-cause at this particular time her system is sluggish, and the sebaceous and sweat-gland pores of the scalp — being inactive — fail to prevent the chemicals from entering as is their duty under normal circum-stances.

J. Howard Crum
The Truth About Beauty (1933) 263

A paste of bisulphate of magnesia and lime is very effectual for bleaching the hair; but it must be used with great caution not to burn hair, skin, and brains together.

S.D.P.
The Ugly Girl Papers (1874) 264

he rage for light, gold-color, or even red hair, which has prevailed for some time, has led to various expedients for procuring it. Many ladies have sacrificed fine heads of hair, and in place of their own dark tresses have adopted light wigs; but the prevailing absurdity has been the use of strong alkalies for the purpose of turning the dark hair light. This is the purpose of the auricomus fluid, which may be procured of any hair-dresser; but we warn our fair readers that the use of these products is apt to be disappointing. They certainly will turn black to a brickdust hue, but the color is often disagreeable; it is apt to present itself in patches of different hues, and the effect on the hair is terrible, it often rots and crumbles away. In place of this absurd practice, we recommend the following as available for trying the effect at a ball or other entertainment — for dress purposes, in short: — Procure a packet of gold powder of the hair-dresser. Have ready a very weak solution of gum and water, and one of the small perfume vaporizers now in use. When the hair has been dressed, sprinkle it with the gum-water, by means of the vaporizer, and then shower on the gold powder. It may be put on thick enough to hide the color of the hair, and, owing to the gum, cannot be danced off.

Author Unknown
Personal Beauty, in *Perfect Etiquette* (187?) 47

Scalp Massage Machine

Face

P hotographs from a century ago show women blissfully free of makeup, presenting their clean, honest faces to the camera and to history.

At first glance, it may seem they were more secure and self-accepting than many of today's women, who wouldn't be caught dead in the supermarket without eyeliner.

But looks can be deceiving. When it came to the darkness of their eyelashes or the smoothness of their skin, it seems a lot of these women were just as crazy as we are — without the benefit of the modern cosmetics counter.

Look at the woman in that old photograph again. Perhaps she's singed her eyelashes. Her eyebrows could be enhanced by sage. Maybe her skin has been smoothed by applications of lettuce or lemon juice, or perhaps her pained expression is the result of having tried the turpentine treatment.

Regardless of her simple appearance, there were plenty of written recommendations emphasizing the same features we seek to enhance today: advice on the quest for the shapely eyebrow, the unblemished complexion, the small nose.

In past eras, even attitude and activities were considered influences on beauty. Thoughts were believed to affect wrinkles and the shape of the nose, while the stress of work was thought to diminish the beauty of the eyes.

Loveliness was serious business to the woman of yesteryear. As one source noted, beauty was important to maintaining a husband — and husbands were important to many women's survival.

So the next time you poke your eye with a mascara wand, just remember — it could be a lot worse.

Motivation

I know not what ails female youth, but seeing what they do, one would believe they took an interest in the definite triumph of ugliness.

Ernest Feydeau
The Art of Pleasing (1877) 57

It is a woman's business to be beautiful.

"S.D.P."
The Ugly Girl Papers (1874) 10

In neglecting your own physical charm, you are encouraging lack of interest in your husband.

Florence Courtenay
Physical Beauty (1922) 10

en, themselves, like to tell us that they consider the spiritual and mental companionship to be the important part of a love between two people, that they would love us just as much were we ugly instead of so beautiful. Perhaps at the time they believe it. Perhaps the women to whom they tell it also believe it. But it is not true.

And this proves the importance, the seriousness of your efforts to develop and keep beauty...

Men's senses take in everything about a woman's appearance, just automatically. A gesture lacking grace, a straggly lock of hair, a blemish on the skin, unconsciously... or consciously... revolt him.

We now see why a woman literally MUST make and keep herself as attractive as possible, physically.

She must constantly please the senses of the man she loves, with her beauty and refinement... her absolute deliciousness! Then she will keep him!

Marjorie Oelrichs
Home Beauty Course (1927) 94-95

Contradictions

Beauty is a dangerous gift... Like wealth it has ruined thousands. Thousands of the most beautiful women are destitute of common sense and common humanity... In about nine cases in ten it makes her silly, senseless, thoughtless, giddy, vain, proud, frivolous, selfish, low and mean.

B.G. Jefferis and J.L. Nichols
Search Lights on Health (1902) 27

The painted face, the brazen look, the plucked eyebrow, the indecent dress which we see now may attract men's eyes but never his heart.

John Carrara
Enemies of Youth (1939) 24

Eyelashes

The eyelashes are important in their influence upon the beauty and appearance of the eye. They may be improved by the practice of gentle pulling, thus stimulating their growth and giving them strength.

Frank Scholl
Library of Health, Vol. II (1916) 1643

The beauty of the eyelashes consists chiefly in their length and silkiness. These qualities may be promoted by occasionally "topping" them with a pair of sharp scissors. The practice is most effective when commenced in early childhood. The least possible portion of their extremities should be removed; and the operation, to be neatly done, must be performed by a second person.

Monfort B. Allen and Amelia C. McGregor
The Glory of Woman (1896) 424-425

You can, however, singe your eyelashes… Simply take a heavy wire hairpin, bend it out straight, embed one end of it firmly in a cork, and then hold the other end in a flame. Wipe any paint off of this carefully with paper before you attempt to singe your eyelashes with it. And don't do this at all unless you are quite sure that your hands are steady enough to attempt it, because you can get a very nasty burn from it and even injure your eyeball badly.

Dare Frances
Lovely Ladies: The Art of Being a Woman
(1929) 224

Grow-

Yes, Grow Eyelashes and Eyebrows like this in 30 Days

Marvelous new discovery!—makes eyelashes and eyebrows *actually grow!* Now as never before you can positively have long, curling, silken lashes and beautiful, wonderful eyebrows.

I say to you in plain English that no matter how scant your eyelashes and brows, I will increase their length and thickness in 30 days—or not accept one penny. No "ifs", "ands" or "maybes"—you actually see startling results—or no pay! You be the judge.

Over 10,000 Women Prove It
—prove beyond a doubt that this astounding new discovery fringes the eyes with long, curling natural lashes—makes eyebrows lovely, silken lines. Read what they say—sworn to under oath before a notary public. From Mlle. Hefflefinger, 240 W., "B" St., Carlisle, Pa.; "I certainly am delighted … people now remark how long and silky my eyelashes appear." From Naomi Otstot, 5437 Westminster Ave., W. Philadelphia, Pa.; "I am greatly pleased. My eyebrows and lashes are beautiful now." Frances Raviart of Jeanette, Pa., says: "Your Eyelash and Eyebrow Beautifier is simply marvelous." Flora J. Corriveau, Biddeford, Me., says "With your Method my eyelashes are growing long and luxurious."

Results Evident In One Week
In one week—often in a day or so—you see the lashes become more beautiful, like silken fringe! The darling little upward curl shows itself and eyebrows become sleek. It's the thrill of a lifetime—when you have lashes and brows as beautiful as any ever seen. Remember—I guarantee you satisfactory results in 30 days—or your money refunded in full. I mean just that—no quibble, no strings.

Send today. Special Introductory Price only $1.95 NOW! Later $5.00. Order NOW at low price.

Lucille Young

Sent C. O. D.—*Or if money accompanies order postage will be prepaid.*

Lucille Young, 6414 Lucille Young Bldg., Chicago,
Send me your new discovery for growing eyelashes and eyebrows. If not entirely satisfied, I'll return it in 30 days and you refund my money.
Price C. O. D. $1.95 plus few cents postage
If $1.95 sent with order postage will be paid.
Check if money enclosed ☐ or C. O. D. ☐

Name..
St. Address......................................
City................State......................

A stick of India ink is perhaps the best method of darkening the eyelashes if that is thought desirable.

Or burnt cork is sometimes employed.

Or cloves charred to a crisp in an open flame.

Sidney Morse
Household Discoveries (1913) 602

As an impromptu expedient to serve for one night — say while staying at a country house — a hair-pin held for a few seconds in the flame of a candle, and drawn through the lashes, will serve to color them well, and with sufficient durability. We need scarcely add that the hair-pin must be suffered to grow cold before used, or the consequence may be that no eyelash will be left to color.

Author Unknown
Personal Beauty, in *Perfect Etiquette* (187?) 14

There are many women who deplore the fact that they lack beautiful brilliant eyes. Their eyes are dull and do not seem to attract much attention. Some women, in the attempt to make their eyes sparkle, treat them with drug-store concoctions and ruin them. Others are foolish enough to apply black pastes to their eyelashes in the attempt to make their eyes appear larger and more attractive. These women are criminals.

John Hewins Kern
Glorious Womanhood (1925) 61

Eyes

Egyptian women make their eyes lovely and lustrous by a wash of strong, black tea.

Georges A. Sakele
One Thousand and One Beauty Hints (1931) 28

In ancient Rome, the ladies of the demi-monde ... took a little belladonna (hence the name) as well, so that the pupils of the eyes should become as large as possible.

J. Rutgers
How To Attain and Practice the Ideal Sex Life (1940) 86

The greatest menace to a business girl's beauty is that of eye strain. The danger that this eye strain will produce wrinkles between her eyebrows, will inflame the lids and cause the eyelashes to fall out, and will dim the brightness of the eyes and produce the tired expression of the old or of those who are devitalized by age or overwork is great.

Lina Cavalieri
My Secrets of Beauty (1914) 54

What girl does not know that eating lump-sugar wet with Cologne just before going out will make her eyes bright, or that the homelier mode of flirting soap-suds into them has the same effect? Spanish ladies squeeze orange juice into their eyes to make them shine.

S.D.P.
The Ugly Girl Papers (1874) 245

Without moving the head, look as far to the left and right as possible; as far up and as far down as possible; diagonally upward right and downward left, and upward left and downward right; roll the eyes in circles, left and right, making as large circles as possible. After doing these exercises with the eyes open, repeat with the eyes closed; then repeat while shutting the eyes tightly. Practise looking cross-eyed. Look upward as far as possible to the right, then as far upward as possible to the left, then zigzag back and forth while progressively lowering the eyes until looking as far downward as possible; then reverse the movement. Do the same exercise by raising and lowering the eyes, traveling across from right to left, then reverse the direction. Imagining a spiral line on the wall, start in the center and circle the eyes, gradually enlarging the circle until the limit of motion is reached; then reverse the direction.

Bernarr Macfadden
Home Health Manual (1930) 34

Eyebrows

Five grains of sulphate of quinine dissolved in an ounce of alcohol, will, if applied, cause eyebrows to grow when burned off by the fire.

John H. Young
Our Deportment (1880) 335

Don't pencil your eyebrows; this soon makes them fall out... To darken them use sage tea, with a few drops of alcohol.

Mary Ries Melendy
Vivilore (1904) 156

Some persons have the eyebrows meeting over the nose. This is usually considered a disfigurement, but there is no remedy for it. It may be a consolation for such people to know that the ancients admired this style of eyebrows, and that Michael Angelo possessed it. It is useless to pluck out the uniting hairs; and if a depilatory is applied, a mark like that of a scar left from a burn remains, and is more disfiguring than the hair.

John H. Young
Our Deportment (1880) 352

Complexion

It is easy to do the complexion irreparable injury in Summer. One too long fishing jaunt, one automobile dash with the skin ill protected against the burning sun; a too long dawdling on the toasting sands, and the evil is done. The once beautiful complexion has become a memory. In its place is only a dry, withered remnant ...

Mme. Lina Cavalieri
My Secrets of Beauty (1914) 14

Occasionally, say once a month, a teaspoon of milk with about one-third the quantity of salt applied to the face just before retiring is a splendid remedy for rough or blotched skin. This may smart a trifle at first, but the face will have a delightful, velvety feeling in the morning.

Alice M. Long
My Lady Beautiful (1906) 200

osmetic juice. — Make a hole in a lemon, fill it with sugar-candy, and close it with leaf gold, applied over the rind that was cut out; then roast the lemon in hot ashes. When desirous of using the juice, squeeze out a little through the hole already made and with it wash the face with a napkin. This juice is said to cleanse the skin and brighten the complexion wonderfully.

Emily Thornwell
The Lady's Guide to Perfect Gentility (1856) 27

e know of one beautiful lady who has not washed her face for three years, yet it is always clean, rosy, sweet, and kissable. With some of her other secrets she gave it to her lover for safe keeping. Unfortunately, it proved to be her last gift to that gentleman, who declared in a subsequent note that "I cannot reconcile my heart and my manhood to a woman who can get along without washing her face."

Georgene Corry Benham
Polite Life and Etiquette (1902) 330-331

Wrinkles

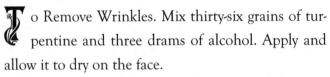

T o Remove Wrinkles. Mix thirty-six grains of turpentine and three drams of alcohol. Apply and allow it to dry on the face.

Walter R. Houghton et al.
American Etiquette and Rules of Politeness (1884) 409

W hen a woman is discontented and harbors grudges, wrinkles are sure to appear.

Monsieur Georges A. Sakele
One Thousand and One Beauty Hints (1931) 10

T he milky juice of the broken stems of coarse garden lettuce rubbed over the face at night, and washed off in the morning with a solution of ammonia, is highly recommended.

Walter R. Houghton et al.
American Etiquette and Rules of Politeness (1884) 408

N ever fully relax your facial muscles except when in a reclining position... Do not blink your eyes, twist your lips, sniffle or adopt any other facial contortion habit. These form wrinkles prematurely.

Viola and Alexander Swan
Beauty's Question and Answer Dictionary (1931) 104

T ake some clippings of sheep's wool and steep in hot alcohol. It is said that the grease thus obtained is identical with an element found in the human bile.

John Coulter
The New Century Perfect Speaker (1901) 549

Chin(s)

ne chin is enough! Double and triple chins certainly do not add to your facial charm.

Florence Courtenay
Physical Beauty (1922) 32

rubber bandage, placed under the chin and fastened on the side or top of the head, not only holds flesh in place, but, by causing free perspiration, gradually reduces the size....

The rubber throat strap is sometimes used with similar bandages, one over the nose and cheeks, and one over the eyes, brow, and temple, for reducing the flesh of the entire face...

William A. Woodbury
Beauty Culture (1910) 340-341

Throat Strap for Chin Reduction   Face Harness

Facial Exercises

lthough women do not realize it, even frowning is a developer of beauty. It requires only thirteen muscles to produce a smile, but the woman who frowns exercises sixty-five muscles. The woman who frowns in public is by no means an attraction, but the one who wants to be truly beautiful should do considerable frowning in the privacy of her boudoir.

John Hewins Kern
Glorious Womanhood (1925) 1

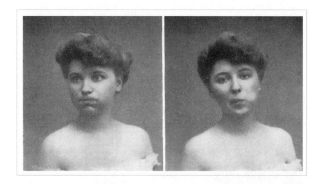

ightly close mouth, then try to force the breath through it. Press the cheeks out as far as possible with tongue.

Bernarr Macfadden
The Power and Beauty of Superb Womanhood
(1901) 176

he problem of cultivating a sweet smile without destroying any of the naturalness of the expression arises at this time, but I assure you it can be done without difficulty.

A simple exercise trains the muscles in their new action. Hold the mouth relaxed and then push out the lips into a soft, elliptical shape. Then raise the center of the upper lip until a tensing of muscles is felt at the corners of the nose. Still retaining as much of this position as possible, draw the corners of the lips back and up... Relax the mouth and repeat twenty times. Do this night and morning and in between times, if you have an opportunity.

In addition to this exercise, you should devote at least five minutes each day to smiling in the new way. This is done by pushing up the center of the upper lip and holding in the corners of the mouth.

Josephine Huddleston
Secrets of Charm (1929) 264

Lips

For the thick lip you may make it appear narrower by remembering never to allow the lips to push out, but hold them in firmly, and use no rouge, which would make them noticeable... a pleasant expression does more than anything else to make people disregard lack of physical perfection.

Ellye Howell Glover
"Dame Curtsey's" Book of Beauty Talks (1923) 13-14

Very excellent Lip-Salve. — Take four ounces of butter, fresh from the churn, cut it small, put it into a jar, cover it with good rose-water, and let it remain for four or five days; then drain it well, and put it into a small and very clean saucepan, with one ounce of spermaceti, and one of yellow beeswax sliced thin, a quarter of an ounce of bruised alkanet root, two drachms of gum benzoin, and one of storax, beaten to powder, half an ounce of loaf sugar, and the strained juice of a moderate sized lemon. Simmer these gently, keeping them stirred all the time, until the mixture looks very clear, and sends forth a fine aromatic odour; then strain it through a thin doubled muslin, and stir to it from twelve to twenty drops of essential oil of roses...

Florence Hartley
Ladies' Book of Etiquette (1873) 318-319

writer whose knowledge of such subjects is beyond question says that glycerine and rose water should never be used to soften the lips, as this remedy has one great drawback, namely, that it induces the growth of superfluous hair, a warning which all women will gladly heed, for no one desires to pose as a bearded lady.

Maud C. Cooke
Manual of Social Forms (1896) 499

he habit of biting the lips soon destroys any grace of form they may have originally possessed. Madame de Pompadour, while lamenting the decay of her charms, confessed that she first began to spoil at the mouth. She had early acquired the habit of biting her lips in order to conceal her emotion.

Author Unknown
The Bazar Book of Decorum (1870) 51

Nose

If a foolish girl, by dint of squeezing and bracing with busk and bones, secures the conventional beauty of a wasp waist, she is tolerably certain to gain an addition she by no means bargained for, a *red nose*... Often, in assemblages of the fair, we have seen noses faultless in form, but tinged with the abhorred hue, to which washes and cosmetics have been applied in wild despair; but in vain! If the lovely owners had known the cause, how speedily the effect would have vanished! for surely the most perverse admirer of a distorted spine and compressed lungs, would deem the acquisition of a dram-drinker's nose, too heavy a condition to be complied with.

Florence Hartley
Ladies' Book of Etiquette (1873) 290-291

It should never be fondled before company, or, in fact, touched at any time, unless absolutely necessary. The nose, like all other organs, augments in size by frequent handling, so we recommend every person to keep his fingers, as well as those of his friends or enemies, away from it.

Aurhor Unknown
The Bazar Book of Decorum (1870) 38

D o not cultivate a scornful attitude toward life in general. It finds its unbeautiful physical reflex in a habitual elevation of the nostrils in a most disagreeable manner.

Florence Courtenay
Physical Beauty (1922) 29

O f course you can't do anything about the bridge, which is the boney part. But if your nose is too broad there because of flesh or if the tip is too fleshy, there's a way to mould that nose to slimmer lines.

With your hands ... covered in cold cream, press firmly on either side of the nose and with slightly less firm pressure rub outwardly along the nose then slightly upward. If the flesh is toward the end, do your rubbing there. Do not pull the skin but be firm. Do this a few minutes each day.

Sylvia of Hollywood
No More Alibis (1935) 90

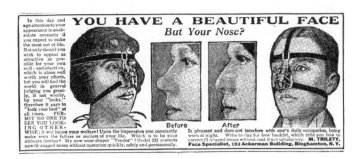

Makeup

At the present day, women paint their eyes, eye-lashes, lips, and even their cheeks, with a powder resembling flour. There are many to be seen daily on the promenade, who use a little carmine on their ears and on the edges of their nostrils. Their faces are dis-gusting, that a respectable man, when he sees them, can feel no other desire than that of washing it.

Ernest Feydeau
The Art of Pleasing (1877) 14

A small red point is made on the inside of the eye-corner and the exposed parts of the nostrils are also painted red. This should be done by a grease-containing preparation, as for example the lip-stick.

Josif Ginsburg
The Hygiene of Youth and Beauty (1926) 97

It is well to use a little pulverized starch when applying the rouge with a rabbit's or hare's foot...

Dr. A. Cazenave
Beauty (1877) 142

No rules can be given for the "just a little powder, just a little paint, making a lady, just what she ain't." We are happy in being able to make ourselves "just what we ain't," for it's what we long to be.

Rebecca
How to be The Smart Woman (1946) 71

Artifice is the main strength of woman.

Monsieur Georges A. Sakele
One Thousand and One Beauty Hints (1931) 21

Bibliography

Allen, Monfort B. and McGregor, Amelia C. The Glory of Woman. 1896.

Anstruther, Elizabeth. The Complete Beauty Book. New York and London: D. Appleton and Company, 1912.

Author Unknown. The Bazar Book of Decorum. New York: Harper & Brothers, 1870.

Author Unknown. The Charm of Fine Manners.Philadelphia: J.B. Lippincott Co., 1920.

Author Unknown. Decorum. New York: Union Publishing House, 1880.

Author Unknown. Good Manners: Reliable Advice on Etiquette Simply Told. L.M. Garrity & Co., 1930.

Author Unknown. How to Woo and How to Win. J. S. Ogilvie Publishing Co., 1919.

Author Unknown. Social Culture. Springfield, Mass.: The King-Richardson Co., 1902.

Author Unknown. The Standard Book on Politeness, Good Behavior and Social Etiquette. New York: M. Young, 1884.

Ayer, Harriet Hubbard. Harriet Hubbard Ayer's Book. Springfield, Mass.: The King-Richardson Co., 1902.

Ayer, Margaret Hubbard. Correct Social Usage. New York: The New York Society of Self-Culture, 1906.

Benham, Georgene Corry. Polite Life and Etiquette. Chicago: Homewood Publishing Co., 1902.

Carrara, John. Enemies of Youth. Grand Rapids, Michigan: Zondervan Publishing House, 1939.

Cavalieri, Lina. My Secrets of Beauty. New York: The Circulation Syndicate, 1914.

Cazenave, Dr. A. Beauty. Cincinnati: Chase & Hall Publishers, 1877.

Chalmers, Leona W. The Intimate Side of a Woman's Life. New York: Pioneer Publications, 1937.

Chesterfield, Lord. Letters, Sentences and Maxims. New York: A.L. Burt Co., n.d.

Chesterfield, Mortimer. Etiquette for Every Occasion. Chicago: Shrewesbury Publishing Co., 1916.

Cooke, Maud C. Manual of Social Forms. Chicago: W.S. Reeve Publishing Co., 1896.

Coulter, John. The New Century Perfect Speaker with Etiquette of Home, Social, Public and Official Life, 1901.

Courtenay, Florence. Physical Beauty: How to Develop and Preserve It. New York: Social Culture Publications, 1922.

Crane, Utley E., ed. New Outline of Knowledge, Vol. X. Philadelphia: Progressive Publishing Company, 1936.

Crum, J. Howard. The Truth About Beauty. New York: Dodd, Mead & Company, 1933.

Derstine, Clayton. Paths to Beautiful Womanhood. Grand Rapids, Michigan: Zondervan Publishing House, 1944.

Feydeau, Ernest. The Art of Pleasing. Cincinnati: Chase & Hall Publishers, 1877.

Fowler, A. L. Fowler's Blue Book of Selected Household Helps, 3rd ed. New York: Household Publishing Co., 1925.

Frances, Dare. Lovely Ladies: The Art of Being a Woman, Vol. I. Garden City, N.Y.: Doubleday, Doran & Co., 1929.

A Gentleman. The Laws of Etiquette. Philadelphia: Lindsay & Blakiston, 1844.

Gibson, Prof. and Mrs. J.W. Social Purity. Naperville, Illinois: J. L. Nichols & Co., 1903.

Ginsburg, Josif. The Hygiene of Youth and Beauty. Los Angeles: Glover, Youth and Beauty Publishing Co., 1926.

Glover, Ellye Howell. "Dame Curtsey's" Book of Beauty Talks. Chicago: A.C. McClurg & Co., 1923.

Glover, Ellye Howell. "Dame Curtsey's" Book of Etiquette. Chicago: Shrewesbury Publishing Co., 1930.

Hadida, Sophia C. Manners for Millions. New York: Doubleday, Doran & Company, 1935.

Hartley, Florence. Ladies' Book of Etiquette. Boston: J.S. Locke & Company, 1873.

Hoffer, Donna Louise. How to Be A Fashion Model. 1940.

Homans, James E. New American Encyclopedia of Social and Commercial Information. New York: P.F. Collier & Son, 1905.

Horton, Thomas D. What Men Don't Like About Women. New York: Louis Greenfield, 1945.

Houghton, Walter R. American Etiquette and Rules of Politeness. New York and Atlanta: John S. Willey Publishing Co., 1884.

Huddleston, Josephine. Secrets of Charm. Scranton, PA: Women's Institute of Domestic Arts & Sciences, 1929.

Jefferis, B.G. and Nichols, J.L. Search Lights on Health. Atlanta: J.L. Nichols, 1902.

Kaji, Hilda M. and Lois Leeds. Beauty and Health: A Practical Handbook. Philadelphia: J. B. Lippincott Co., 1927.

Kern, John Hewins. Glorious Womanhood. New York: Charles Renard Corp. Publishers, 1925.

A Lady of New York. Etiquette for Ladies. Philadelphia: J. & J.L. Gihon, 1843.

Lane, Harriet. The Book of Culture. New York: Social Culture Publications, 1922.

Law, Hartland and Herbert E. Viavi Hygiene. San Francisco: The
Viavi Company, 1902.Laynard, Boyd. Secrets of Beauty, Health
and Long Life. London: Hammond, Hammond & Co., 1905.

Livingston, Margaret Watts. Correct Social Usage. New York: The
New York Society of Self-Culture, 1906.

Long, Alice M. My Lady Beautiful. Chicago: The Progress Company,
1906.

Macfadden, Bernarr. Beauty and Health: A Magazine for Women, vol.
XIII. New York: Physical Culture Publications, May 1908.

Macfadden, Bernarr. Home Health Manual. New York: Macfadden
Book Co., 1930.

Macfadden, Bernarr. The Power and Beauty of Superb Womanhood.
New York: Physical Culture Publishing Co., 1901.

Martens, Frederick H. The Book of Good Manners. New York: Social
Culture Publications, 1923.Martine, Arthur. Martine's Handbook of Etiquette. New York: Dick & Fitzgerald, 1866.

McLeod, Edyth Thornton. Your Home Guide to Health, Beauty,
Charm. New York: Archway Press, 1947.

Melendy, Mary Ries. Vivilore: The Pathway to Mental and Physical
Perfection. W.R. Vasant, 1904.

Miller, Annie Jenness. Physical Beauty: How to Obtain and Preserve
It. (New York: Jenness Miller Monthly, 1894.

Morris, Charles. The Standard Book of Etiquette. 1901.

Morse, Sidney. Household Discoveries. Petersburg, N.Y.: Success
Company, 1913.

Morton, Agnes H. Etiquette. Philadelphia: The Penn Publishing Co.,
1895.

N.C. Practical Etiquette. Chicago: A. Flanagan Co., 1899.

Northrop, Henry Davenport. The Household Encyclopedia. Boston:
Desmond Publishing Co., 189?.

Oerlrichs, Marjorie. Home Beauty Course. Boncilla Laboratories,
1927.

Ordway, Edith B. The Etiquette of Today. New York: George Sully
and Company, 1920.

Rebecca. How to be The Smart Woman. Richmond: The Dietz Press,
1946.

Robinson, William J. Woman: Her Sex and Love Life. New York:
Eugenics Publishing Co., 1938.

Rosen, Carl. The Face, Hair and Scalp. 1906.

Sakele, Monsieur Georges A. One Thousand and One Beauty Hints.
New York: Poetic Publications, Inc., 1931.

Sangster, Margaret. Good Manners for All Occasions. New York:
Cupples & Leon Co., 1904.

Scholl, Frank. Library of Health, vol. II B. Philadelphia: American Health Society, 1916.S.D.P. The Ugly Girl Papers. New York: Harper & Brothers, 1874.

Shannon, T.W. Eugenics. Marietta, Ohio: The S.A. Mullikin Co., 1919.

Shannon, T.W. Perfect Womanhood. Ohio: S.A. Mullikin Company, 1913.

Smith, Frances. Talks with Homely Girls. New York: A.L. Burt, 1886.

A Society Lady. How to Acquire Personal Beauty. Chicago: R. S. Peale & Co., 1889.

Starrett, Helen Ekin. The Charm of Fine Manners. Philadelphia: J.B. Lippincott Co., 1920.

Swan, Alexander and Viola. Beauty's Question and Answer Dictionary. Hollywood: Beauty Arts Institute, 1931.

Sylvia of Hollywood. No More Alibis! Chicago: Photoplay Publishing Co., 1934.

Sylvia of Hollywood. Pull Yourself Together, Baby! New York: Macfadden Book Company, 1936.

Sylvia of Hollywood. Streamline Your Figure. New York: Macfadden Book Co., 1939.

Thompson, Alice and Valentine, Helen. Better Than Beauty: A Guide to Charm. New York: Modern Age Books, 1938.

Thornwell, Emily. The Lady's Guide to Perfect Gentility. New York: Derby & Jackson, 1856.

Turner, Albert. Womanly Beauty of Form and Feature. New York: The Health-Culture Company, 1900.

Warren, Mrs. Jane. Ladies' Own Home Cook Book. New York: Hurst & Company, 1891.

Wells, Richard A. Manners, Culture and Dress. Springfield, MA: King, Richardson & Co., 1891.

White, Annie Randall. Twentieth Century Etiquette. Chicago: The L. W. Walter Company, 1903.

Whitehead, C.S. and Hoff, Charles A. The New Eugenics. Chicago: The John A. Hertel Co., 1932.

Wilson, Margery. Charm. New York: Frederick A. Stokes Company, 1928.

Wilson, Margery. The Pocket Book of Etiquette. New York: Pocket Books, 1940.

Wolf, Annie. The Truth About Beauty. New York: Lovell, Coryell & Company, 1892.

Woodbury, William A. Beauty Culture. New York: G.W. Dillingham Company, 1910.

Young, John H. Our Deportment. Detroit: F.B. Dickerson & Co., 1880.

Index

Internet Resources

Five favorite sites for finding
antiquarian books online

AcqWeb: Rare and Antiquarian Book Vendors
Start here for a directory of online booksellers specializing in a wide variety of subjects.
http: acqweb.library.vanderbilt.edu/
acqweb/pubr/rare.html

Advanced Book Exchange
This site lets you search the catalogs of over
10,000 booksellers at once.
http://www.abebooks.com

Alibris
Browsable by subject, with separate catego-
ries for first-edition and signed books.
http://www.alibris.com

Book Finder
Includes international booksellers and over
40 million books.
http://www.bookfinder.com

Ebay
Start with the "Books: Antiquarian & Col-
lectible" category. You never know what you might
find!
http://www.ebay.com

About the Author

Monica Dale, a professional dancer, pianist, and author of the *Eurhythmics for Young Children* series, has been fascinated by antiquated ideas on beauty, charm, and etiquette since she was a skinny 13-year old watching Scarlett O'Hara being laced into a corset.

Monica shares her Art Deco-furnished home with an extensive collection of antiquarian books, along with an eccentric array of antique hats, gloves, and purses. Her idea of a good time is an afternoon perusing flea markets, an evening at an antiques auction, or a few hours regaling her friends with quotes from her book collection. Their enthusiastic responses were the impetus for *Advice from the Attic*.

Monica lives in a Baltimore suburb with her daughter Hilary and husband Michael, who's forever building new bookshelves to accommodate her growing collection of "weird old books."

To arrange author's speaking engagements and book signings, contact:

Monica Dale
Fax: 410-465-8472
Email: monicadale@hatpinpress.com

It would be *highly improper* for you to miss any new books ...

Visit Hatpin Press

www.hatpinpress.com